William M Berger

Berger's Tourists' Guide to New Mexico

Including Descriptions of Towns, Pueblos, Churches, Pictures, Statues...

William M Berger

Berger's Tourists' Guide to New Mexico
Including Descriptions of Towns, Pueblos, Churches, Pictures, Statues...

ISBN/EAN: 9783337003883

Printed in Europe, USA, Canada, Australia, Japan

Cover: Foto ©Andreas Hilbeck / pixelio.de

More available books at **www.hansebooks.com**

—— to ——

NEW MEXICO,

—— INCLUDING ——

DESCRIPTIONS OF TOWNS, PUEBLOS, CHURCHES, PICTURES, STATUES, RUINS AND ANTIQUITIES; TOGETHER WITH MOUNTAINS, CAÑONS, SPRINGS, AND OTHER PLACES OF INTEREST.

WM. M. BERGER,
SANTA FE.

KANSAS CITY, MO.:
PUBLISHING HOUSE OF RAMSEY, MILLETT & HUDSON.
1883.

LA VETA PASS, ON THE LINE OF THE DENVER & RIO GRANDE R. R.

Bookseller Stationer

FIRST NATIONAL BANK BUILDING,

Santa Fe,   New Mexico.

VIEWS

OF NEW MEXICO AND THE GREAT SOUTHWEST,

Souvenir Albums

— A N D —

Medals San Miguel Church, Stationery, Fancy Articles,

ETC., ETC., ETC.

INTRODUCTORY.

This little book is intended for a "TOURIST'S GUIDE" to New Nexico, drawing attention to such objects in each place as are best worthy of the attention of the traveller; and it does not attempt to give the history, or any full description of the natural resources or business opportunities of the Territory; they would be out of place here. The history can be found in books specially on that subject, and those wishing information as to resources, products, and business matters, can obtain them from the Bureau of Immigration, or the score of excellent land agencies that exist in the Territory. We only propose, before proceeding to the special descriptions of places, to give a few general facts as to characteristic features and history, sufficient to make the particular descriptions more intelligible; and to add a small chapter on the pronunciation of Spanish names, which is peculiarly desirable in this Territory.

General Features.

New Mexico is a great Plateau, traversed by mountain ranges, and increasing in elevation from south to north. Scarcely anywhere is its elevation less than 4,000 feet—at Santa Fé it is over 7,000; and its highest peaks are nearly 13,000. The most peculiar feature of its landscapes are the *mesas*, or tables, being elevations with perfectly flat tops; sometimes quite small, and sometimes extending for many miles, but always with this feature, unknown in most lands, of the perfectly level top; which is usually caused by a stratum of some solid rock. These will be seen under ever-varying circumstances in all parts of the Territory. The total area is 121,201 square miles, the Territory being about 335 miles from east to west, 345 miles from north to south at the east boundary, and 390 at the west. The population in 1880, exclusive of Indians, who are not citizens, was 119,565; of whom 64,496 were male, and 55,069 female; 111,514 native, and 8,051 foreign; 108,721 white, and 10,844 colored, the latter including Pueblo Indians and half-breeds. The population has increased very rapidly since the coming of the railroads, the total in 1883 exceeding 150,000.

The climate is considered the finest in the United States. The high altitude insures dryness and purity, and by travelling from place to place almost any desired temperature can be enjoyed. The elevations of some of the principal points are as follows: Santa Fé, 7,047; Old Fort Marcy, 7,340; Costilla, 7,774; Tierra Amarilla, 7,455; Glorieta, 7,587; Taos, 6,950; Las Vegas, 6,452; Cimarron, 6,489; Bernalillo, 5,704; Albuquerque, 4,918; Socorro, 4,655; Las Cruces, 3,844; Silver City, 5,946; Ft. Stanton, 5,800. The mean temperature at the Government Station at Santa Fé, for several years, was as follows: 1874, 48.9 degrees; 1875, 48.6; 1876, 48.1; 1877, 48.3; 1878, 47.6; 1879, 50.6; 1880, 46.6; which shows an extraordinary uniformity. For tubercular diseases the death rate in New Mexico is the lowest in the country, the ratio being as follows: New England, 25; Minnesota, 14; Southern States, 6; and New Mexico, 3.

The first thing which strikes the stranger is the material and style of the houses, they being generally of *adobe* (a-do′bay), and one story high. An adobe is a sun-dried brick, moulded of earth and straw, and usually 18x9x4. They are the same bricks which the Children of Israel were called on to make in Egypt, and which are the general building material in dry countries the world over. Some "tenderfeet," especially correspondents who write learnedly of the whole Territory after being within it for a day, think it brilliant to refer to the adobe houses as "mud" houses; forgetting that with as much propriety might the stores and residences of Philadelphia be called "clay houses," because their bricks happen to be made of that variety of earth. A short residence teaches the new-comer, that for this climate, no house is so entirely comfortable as one with thick adobe walls, to keep it cool in summer and warm in winter. They were usually built in a square around a court, called a *placita*, with one large entrance or *saguan*; all the rooms opening upon this court. Originally they had few windows on the outside, but now these are added. The roofs are flat, supported by round timbers called *vigas*, on which are laid boards,

NEW MEXICO

REAL × ESTATE × AND × INSURANCE × AGENCY.

JESSE M. WHEELOCK,

AGENT FOR

BACA ADDITION. BACA & ARMIJO ADDITION, PEREA ADDITION,
NICOLAS T. ARMIJO ADDITION, EASTERN ADDITION,
And Numerous Lots in NEW MEXICO TOWN COMPANY'S Town Site.

ARCHITECT and SUPERINTENDENT. PLANS and SPECIFICATIONS FURNISHED.

Offices in Cromwell Block,

Albuquerque, - - - - New Mexico.

H. W. WYMAN,

—DEALER IN—

Metallic & Wood Coffins & Caskets,

And Undertakers' Supplies.

EMBALMING A SPECIALTY.

ALL ORDERS BY TELEGRAPH PROMPTLY ATTENDED TO.

Las Vegas, N. M.

HISTORICAL SOCIETY
—OF—
New Mexico.

Rooms, Washington Ave., between the Palace and Palace Hotel,

Santa Fe, New Mexico.

HON. L. BRADFORD PRINCE, President.
EUGENE A. FISKE, Vice-President.
DAVID J. MILLER, Cor. Secretary.
WILLIAM M BERGER, Rec. Secretary.
S. SPIEGELBERG, Treasurer.
JOHN C. PEARCE, Curator.

Strangers are Cordially Invited to Visit the Rooms.

which are covered with earth, the top of which is worked over so as to shed water. Inside, the rooms are whitewashed with a kind of gypsum called "yezo," which is dazzlingly white; and the lower part of the walls, the fire-place, etc., are usually coated with *tierra amarilla*, which is yellow in color, and glistening with specks of mica, and which will not rub off, as the "yezo" will. The fire-places are usually in the corner of rooms, and it may be mentioned here, that the wood is burned *upright*, which is much better on many accounts than the horizontal position common elsewhere.

In every town, large or small, is a church or chapel, generally the only lofty building in the place, which, if large, is cruciform in shape, and usually has a bell-tower in front. As the roofs are flat, the width of these churches, without regard to their length, is limited by the length of the *vigas*.

Another feature, that always attracts attention, is the abundance of small donkeys, called burros (boor´ro), which are used for almost all purposes by the common people. They carry burdens of astonishing size, of wood, grain, flour, fruit, hay—in fact, anything that is placed upon them—with a patience and perseverance which are remarkable. No street scene in New Mexico is perfect that does not include some of these little animals; and without them it is difficult to see how business could proceed.

Brief Historical Sketch.

The first European to enter New Mexico was Cabeza de Vaca, who was shipwrecked on the coast of Texas, and after long wanderings, extending over several years, reached the western side of the continent in Sonora in 1538. He passed through New Mexico, crossing the Pecos, ascending the Rio Grande for thirty-four days, seeing the permanent buildings of the Pueblo Indians, and being presented with turquoise from the great mine at Cerrillos. In 1539 Friar Marcos de Niza came on an exploring expedition as far as Zuñi, which he called Cibola, but could not enter the city. He gave such a glowing account of the richness of the country that the next year Coronado came with an expedition composed of the flower of the chivalry of Mexico. He came to Zuñi; then to Tiguere and Cicuyé, the principal cities in the valley of the Rio Grande, the former being on the Puerco an the latter near Santa Ana; visited Lagura and Acoma; and thence proceeded across the Great Plains to Quivira, on the Missouri River. A fall from his horse, and the desire to return to his wife, caused Coronado to return in 1542 without permanent colonization.

In 1581 came the expedition of Friar Ruiz and two companions as missionaries; and on December 10, 1582, Don Anito de Espejo started on an expedition to rescue them, but was too late. He explored the country, however, as far west as Zuñi and Moqui, and north to the vicinity of Santo Domingo.

In 1591 Juan de Oñate led a colony which settled at the mouth of the Chama River, and within a few years the whole country was populated by Spaniards. He made an expedition to Quivira in 1599. By 1608 8,000 Indians had been baptized, and by 1629, 34,650.

In 1661 Peñalosa led his famous expedition across the Plains to Quivira, but was soon after imprisoned in Mexico at the instance of the Inquisition. In 1680 the Pueblos, who had been driven to desperation by a practical slavery in the mines, and other ill treatment, revolted and drove the Spaniards from the Territory. They held possession about thirteen years, when Governor Diego de Vargas again reduced the country to Spanish control. During the interim all the churches, etc., had been destroyed, but they were soon after rebuilt.

About 1805 the first trader came from the United States across the Plains, and the business of the Santa Fé Trail increased from that time until the building of the railroad. In 1837 there was a rebellion in the north of the Territory, which was successful for a time, but was finally put down by Gen. Armijo, who became Governor. In 1846, in the "Mexican War," Gen. Kearney marched across the Plains and entered Santa Fé without opposition, taking possession of the whole of New Mexico as United States' territory. A provisional government was established with Charles Bent as Governor; but he was killed in January, 1847, in the Taos Insurrection, which was soon after suppressed by Gen. Price. Since then, with the exception of Indian wars, the Territory has been at peace. In 1879 the railroad arrived at Las Vegas, and since then development has been very rapid.

The Pueblo Indians, the civilized aborigines, are probably an offshoot from the Aztecs who remained here when the main body of the nation migrated to the South.

This little skeleton history is given simply to show the connection between different events mentioned in the descriptions of various localities.

TOLTEC GORGE, BELOW THE TUNNEL.

FIRST

National Bank

-OF-

SANTA FE, NEW MEXICO.

UNITED STATES DEPOSITORY.

Capital,	-	-	-	-	$150,000
Surplus,	-	-	-	-	90,000

S. B. ELKINS,   R. J. PALEN,

     President.   Cashier

      W. W. GRIFFIN, Vice-President.

DIRECTORS:

S. B. ELKINS,   PEDRO PEREA,   T. B. CATRON,

    W. W. GRIFFIN,   R. H. LONGWILL.

LOUIS SULZBACHER,   R. J. PALEN.

Pronunciation of Spanish Names.

These names are so constantly met with, in New Mexico, that it is desirable, of course, to pronounce them correctly. Fortunately, no language is so easy to pronounce as Spanish—a few brief rules include the whole subject. Every letter has an unvarying sound, and the accents, unless specially designated in the word, are uniform and unchanging. So that a person seeing a printed word knows instantly how it is pronounced; and one hearing a spoken word, knows exactly how it is spelled. The sounds of the letters are as follows, as nearly as can be easily represented:—

A—as in Ah.

B—as in English.

C—before a, o, or u, is hard, like K.

C—before e and i, is soft like S.

D—as in English.

E—as A.

F—as in English.

G—before a, o, or u, is hard, as G in "go."

G—before e and i, is pronounced like H.

H—is silent.

I —as E.

J—as H.

K—as in English.

L—as in English.

M—as in English.

N—as in English.

O—the full sound as in "go."

P—as in English.

Q—(always followed by "u") as K.

R—as in English.

S—as in English, the sharp sound only, as in "sister."

T—as in English.

U—as Oo, or u in "Ruth."

V—as in English.

W—no such letter.

X—little used now. The J is generally used in preference.

Y—as in English when a consonant, when a vowel, like the Spanish I " E."

Z—like s in "sister."

CH—is always sounded as in English.

In addition to these there are two letters, or combinations, not in English.

LL—is pronounced exactly as L followed by Y, as "Olla," pronounced "Ole-ya."

Ñ—(originally a double n) is pronounced as N followed by Y, as "niño," pronounced "neen-yo."

In *Gue* and *Gui* the "u" only has the effect of making the sound of the G hard; as Gay and Ghee.

It is proper to add that in Castile, the soft C and the Z are pronounced TH (as in "thin"), but in all Spanish America, as well as most of Spain, they are pronounced as "S;" and it appears like affectation to sound them otherwise. So in some places the D has a slight lisping sound added to it, but not sufficiently generally to make it worth while to try to imitate it, at any rate until experienced in the language.

The above are all the sounds, and are absolutely invariable. By simply taking any Spanish word and pronouncing the letters, *every one*, just as they come, as above, you will be sure to be right.

Remember a few things: *There are no dipthongs in Spanish.* That is, two vowels are never pronounced as one sound; each one has its own sound—thus "Eugenio" is Ai-oo hay nee-o, the first two letters being as separate as any others. The nearest approach to a dipthong is where ao are together, producing nearly the sound of "ow" in English; or ai, producing nearly the sound of "i" in English; but a moment's examination will show that each letter preserves its sound. *There is no sound of "sh" or "zh," like the English sounds in "shall" and "usual." There are no such vowel sounds as e in "pet," i in "pin," a in "fat," o in "hot," u in "utter," oo in "wood" (same as u in "bull"), or as au or aw in "slaughter" and "law." There is no "z" sound, ever. There is no "j" or soft "g" sound.* Remembering this will save many mistakes.

The accentuation is very simple. In all singular nouns ending with a consonant the accent is on the last syllable; if ending with a vowel, on the syllable before the last. But note that in Spanish two vowels coming together are for this purpose counted as one syllable; so that *Tapia* is pronounced "Tah'pee-ah," and not "Tah-pee'ah." Words pluralized by adding "es" do not change the accent on account of that addition. All words varying from these rules, except a few common names, and the regular parts of some verbs, have special accents upon them. With the above rules, the traveller can pronounce absolutely correctly every word that he sees.

In New Mexico, in the course of long years, when she was practically cut off from the mother country, and her language was only a spoken one, handed down from father to son, without any standard of revision, some corruptions naturally crept in; the only wonder being that they are so few. These are all, as might be expected, in the direction of carelessness, or of slurring sounds, or dropping them; in short, what might be called "labor-saving" changes. We mention the principal ones of these for the double purpose of having the tourist avoid them, and also that he may understand what is meant by a name if he hears it in its corrupted form. First, the use of B for V or V for B. This shows itself more in writing or print than in speaking; but the mistake in spelling comes from a corruption in pronunciation. Thus we see "Begas" for "Vegas;" "Balencia" for "Valencia;" "Bermejo" for "Vermejo," etc. Second, the dropping of the "l" sound from "ll." This is a most aggravating error, as it loses to the language that liquid sound which is the special charm of Italian, Portuguese, Spanish, and the other languages of Southern Europe. But the truth remains that most of the uneducated New Mexicans drop the "l" completely, and pronounce "ll" as if it were "y." Thus, the traveller will hear Bernalillo pronounced "Bernaliyo;" Gallegos, "Gayegos;" Mesilla, "Mesiya;" Valles, "Vayes;" Cerrillos, "Cerriyos;" villa as if "via;" olla as if "oya," and amarilla as if "amaria;" in fact, so much had the name of Tierra Amarilla been shortened down by this labor-saving process, that it appears in one official document spelled "Tia Maria." In some cases the two cases of corruption just mentioned are united with very startling effect, as when "caballo" is metamorphosed into "cavayo," and "cebolla" into "sevoya." The writer has seen "bueyes" spelled "vuelles," and "yo"—the consonant of words —spelled "llo." Third, the dropping of the "D" sound (which should be very strongly accentuated) in the syllable "ado," at the end of words; thus giving it the English sound of "ow" in "cow." This, of course, is not among educated people, but it is mentioned because the traveller may hear "Colorow" for "Colorado," "Delgow" for "Delgado," "low" for "lado," etc.; and be at a loss to understand what is meant. Fourth, another corruption, not so general, is in the dropping of the sound of "G" when it precedes "ua;" and so miscalling so common a word as "ague" as if it was "awa;" "Guadalupe," "Wadalupe;" "Guadalajara," "Wadalajara;" "Gudymas," "Wymas" etc. It is difficult to see how people fell into the habit of

WM. A. McKENZIE,

dropping these letters, unless from sheer laziness; but it seemed proper to mention it, lest the traveller, who knows some Spanish, should be nonplused by hearing some one say "awa," or talk of Our Lady of "Wadalupe."   For these corruptions are not confined to natives, but just as a Chinaman learns American oaths before any other words, so some "Americans" seem to think it shows a great proficiency in the language to use these corruptions, which the excellent schools in the Territory will soon make things of the past.   There is one corruption, far worse than any of these, which we trust the tourist will not come across, unless perhaps among the Pueblo Indians—that is the dropping of the "B" in "Bueno" and saying "Waino;" that can only be compared to the other Pueblo corruption of "mucho" into "muncho.'

Of course these peculiarities are not general, and when we consider the long isolation of New Mexico, and the general lack of education during more than a century they are very few.

SANTA · FE.

Santa Fé, the City of the Holy Faith of St. Francis, by far the oldest capital in the United States, is also its most ancient city. Long before Cabeza de Vaca roamed across New Mexico, or Colorado unlocked the mysteries of the Land of the Seven Cities, Santa Fé was a flourishing Pueblo town, extending, as the ruins and remains of pottery and stone implements conclusively prove, more than five miles along the valley of the little stream which bears its name.

The history of its first European settlement was lost, with most of the early records of the Territory, by the destruction of all the archives in 1680. But the earliest mention of it shows it even then to have been the capital and the center of authority and influence. Probably the first Spaniards who penetrated into the country after Coronado had opened it to the knowledge of mankind, were attracted by the situation and climate of the old pueblo town, and made it their residence, and even before that time it is likely that the good Friar Luis, who insisted on remaining when Coronado retired from the country, came over from his home near Zia, and preached Christianity to the people. We only learn by accident of Oñate's first visit to the town, from its being incidentally stated in speaking of the triumphal entry of Vargas in 1692, that he carried the same colors under which Oñate had marched into Santa Fé a century before. From this city in 1599 Oñate started on his great expedition across the plains to the famed city of Quivira; and to its Plaza came the delegation of Quivirans on their return visit in 1606. Here in 1662 Peñalosa marshaled his magnificent array of chivalry, for a similar venturesome march, and in the Palace he confined the Chief Official of the Inquisition but a year later. On the hills around appeared the Pueblo army of Popé on the 11th of August, 1680, and then ensued the nine days' siege, conducted and resisted with equal gallantry until farther effort being useless the Spaniards evacuated the city and it fell into the hands of its old inhabitants. Then its churches were demolished, all documents and papers and every sacred vessel and image were destroyed by great fires in the Plaza; estufas were constructed, the "cachina" religious dance again performed, and everything possible done to obliterate even the remembrance of foreign domination. Then after twelve years, on September 13, 1692, Vargas, the *Reconquistador*, entered the town but did not remain, and on December 16, 1693, made his final triumphal entry alluded to in the description of the Plaza. On that occasion he found the Taños Indians in possession of the palace, and wishing to conciliate even after his conquest, he encamped the Spanish forces and families on the hills north of the town until Christmas day. Then he demanded the use of the houses for his army and people, and as the Indians had decided not to leave, a desperate though brief siege took place, the battle raging all day on the 26th, followed by the surrender on the 27th, and the speedy execution of all the Pueblo warriors who were taken prisoners, in the Plaza in front of the palace. Here, in 1804, came the first venturesome trader from the East—the fore-runner of the great line of merchants who made the traffic of the "Santa Fé Trail" world-wide in its celebrity. Here, in August, 1837, came Gov. Perez when he found himself unsupported against the rebellion; and here, a few hours after his retreat, the brutal multitude brought his head, and inaugurated the chief of the insurrection, José Gonzales, a Pueblo Indian, as Governor. Here Armijo, in the counter-revolution, established his authority, and here he

caused the ring-leaders in the revolt to be executed. **Here, in** 1846, the same Armijo marched out to meet the American armies, **and** here, a few **days** later, **on** August 18, Gen. Kearney took possession of the palace **and raised the Stars and** Stripes in the **Plaza.** Here, on the 10th of March, 1862, appeared **the forces of the** Southern Confederacy, and established the Rebel rule, which continued until April 8, when they retired toward Texas, and the Union forces returned.

Thus we have rapidly sketched some of the scenes in the history of this Ancient Capital. **By** its side, Jamestown and New Amsterdam and Plymouth forget their antiquity, **and** even St. Augustine loses its old position of priority.

Having said so much of the town **generally, we proceed** to enumerate some of the special **objects** of **interest which tourists usually visit.**

POINTS OF INTEREST.

1. Fort Marcy.—The Tourist should first visit this height, which overlooks the entire city and the surrounding country for a distance of ninety miles. This will give a general idea of the geographical situation; the Rocky Mountains extending along the east; the Cerrillos, Placers, and Sandias rising beyond each other to the south, and the great ranges far beyond the Rio Grande fringing the western horizon. For a special description and history of the Fort, see separate sketch.

It can be reached on foot either from Palace Avenue or Washington Avenue, or directly eastward from the Palace Hotel. An excellent carriage road has been built from Washington Avenue, just north of the Exhibition Grounds. An observatory is erected on the summit, the top of which is 320 feet above the Plaza.

2. The Palace.—This building occupies the entire northern side of the Plaza, and is by far the most interesting edifice, historically, in the United States. A separate sketch is devoted to this building.

3. The Plaza.—This park, according to the universal custom in Spanish-American towns, occupies the centre of the city. Around it cluster the most important business houses, as well as the Palace and other points of historic interest. Down to the American occupation it was an open square, without trees; filled with wagons, horses, burros, etc., and the scene of a large proportion of the business of the town. Here came, each year, the great caravans of the traders of the Santa Fé Trail, amid the greatest excitement. Into this Plaza, in 1591, Oñate marched with his banners flying; and on the 16th of December, 1693, the people were drawn up, the men on one side and the women on the other, to witness the triumphal entry of Vargas. On this latter occasion the troops marched in first, then opened ranks for the priests to pass through, and the latter, on reaching the center of the square, where the Pueblo Indians had erected a great cross, knelt down, chanted the Litany, and then sung the Te Deum.

In 1846 almost the first act of Gen. Kearney on entering the city was to cause a flag pole 100 feet in height to be erected here, and the stars and stripes flung to the breeze from its summit.

The Plaza is now a place of beauty and refreshment. The bright green alfalfa beneath, the waving branches of the cottonwoods overhead, the Monument teaching its lessons of patriotism and gratitude in the centre, the fountains filling the air with brilliant spray, the strains of music from the military band in the Pagoda, the seats covered with people of nearly every nationality, including the European, the African, the Mongolian, and the Indian; all these things unite to make it a charming and attractive place.

4. The Soldiers' Monument, in the Plaza, was erected by the Legislature of the Territory in honor of the soldiers who died in the battles of the rebellion and those against the Indians. The inscriptions on it are:—

East.—" Erected by the People of New Mexico, through their Legislatures of 1866-7-8. May the Union be perpetual."

South.—" To the Heroes of the Federal Army who fell at the battle of Valverde, fought with the rebels February 21, 1862."

West.—" To the Heroes of the Federal Army who fell at the battles of Cañon del Apache and Pigeon's Rancho (La Glorieta), fought with the rebels March 28, 1862, and to those who fell at the battle fought with the rebels at Peralta, April 15, 1862."

North.—" To the Heroes who have fallen in the various battles with savage Indians in the Territory of New Mexico."

5. The Cathedral of St. Francis.—This stands at the east end of San Francisco street, and is the most conspicuous structure in the city. A separate description is devoted to it.

6. St. Vincent Hospital.—This joins the Cathedral grounds to the north, and is a large and imposing edifice. The new building was finished in 1882 and the ornamental fence around the grounds erected in 1883. It is the only hospital of any importance in the Territory, and by an act of the legislature, receives $400 a month from the public treasury for the support of indigent persons requiring medical aid or nursing. It is under the charge of the Sisters of Charity.

7. Church of the Holy Faith (Episcopal) is situated on Palace Avenue, on the high ground which is now the most fashionable locality for building residences. It is a tasteful structure of stone, erected in 1882. The memorial window in it, representing St. Agnes, is said to be the finest specimen of stained glass in the Southwest.

8. Arch-bishop's Garden.—South of the cathedral on the easterly side of the street leading to the river, are the buildings long familiar to both residents and strangers as the residence of Arch-bishop Lamy. Behind the houses is a beautiful garden which he expended many years and much money in bringing to perfection. Trees of all kinds are here found growing luxuriantly, and producing fruit of almost unequalled size and quality. One special attraction in this garden is a pond filled with choice fish, and containing several islands connected by rustic bridges.

A number of other gardens and orchards are found in the city, any of which are well worthy of a visit; the extreme smoothness of bark and thriftiness of fruit-trees in this vicinity being a special subject of remark. The grounds of W. H. Manderfield are particularly noticeable.

9. The Academy of Our Lady of Light.—This and the other buildings belonging to the Sisters of Loreto, are situated on the street leading from the east of the Plaza across the Santa Fé River. The Academy is a large building surrounded by a cupalo, built in 1881, and of imposing appearance. This Sisters' School was established in 1852 by Sister M. Magdalen Hayden, who for thirty years was the Superior, and under whom a whole generation was educated. About twenty-five boarders and 300 day scholars are taught here.

10. The Sisters' Chapel adjoins the Academy, and is a beautiful stone edifice, tasteful in every respect. Near the entrance will be observed a curious white marble tablet representing Our Lady of Light. This was originally in the church on the south side of the Plaza.

Immediately to the south are the buildings in which the Sisters reside. This academy is the mother institution of the Sisters of Loreto in the Territory, other educational establishments having subsequently been established by them at Taos,

SCENE IN THE ROCKY MOUNTAINS, NEW MEXICO.

Mora, Las Vegas, Bernalillo, Socorro, and Las Cruces in New Mexico, and at San Elizario in Texas.

11. Church of San Miguel.—This Church, so celebrated for its an tiquity, is situated on the same street, after crossing the river. It is about 74 feet long, by 30 feet wide, and 35 feet in height. The walls are of adobe, and the roof, like those of all the older churches, is made of vigas supported by carved timbers at each end, the whole being covered with boards and about twelve inches of closely packed earth. In this Church only two of the ancient square vigas remain, the others having been replaced by newer round ones. The Church is supposed to have been built originally very shortly after the year 1600, or possibly even a year or two before, in the time of Oñate. In the Pueblo revolution of 1680 it was, to a great extent, destroyed, although it is believed that the walls still standing are partly those of the original edifice. History records that in December, 1693, soon after the reconquest by Vargas, a number of men were sent to the mountains to cut timber for the repair of this Church, but that they returned in a few days without accomplishing their object, on account of the extreme cold. From this it would appear that the walls were standing, as large timber could only be needed for the vigas. The entire rebuilding of the Church was completed in 1710, as appears from the inscription still plainly legible on the great square viga near the west end of the building, which reads:—

" El Señor Marquez de la Peñuela hiza esta fabrica, el Alferes Real Don Agustin Flores Vergara, su criado. Año de 1710."

" The Marquis de la Peñuela erected this building. The Royal Ensign Don Agustin Flores Vergara, his servant. The year 1710."

Over the altar is a painting of St. Michael and the Dragon; the other two principal pictures in the chancel being of the Annunciation."

12. San Miguel College.—This flourishing institution is in charge of the Christian Brothers, who have not only succeeded in erecting a noble building, but also in imparting a high degree of scholarship to their gratuates. The College is three stories high and surrounded by a high and lofty cupola, from which a very fine view of the city is to be had. The main building is 160x26 feet, and the wings, when finished, will make an important addition. This school has nearly 100 boarders and a large number of day scholars. The Christian Brothers, who are devoted entirely to education, were founded in 1770, and now number 13,000 members.

13. The Old Pueblo House.—The oldest house in the City, which is said to date back beyond the time of the Spanish conquest, and to be the only remaining representative of the original Pueblo dwellings, is situated just north of the San Miguel church, across a narrow street. The house is two stories high—the second story being very low, and the floor between the upper and lower rooms being made of adobe. The building is now thirty feet long and was originally twice that size; but a few years ago the upper story of the eastern portion fell. The first story is eight feet high and the second six feet. One-half of the house belongs to the family of Manuela Armenta and the other to that of Ularia Ensiñas.

14. The South Side Streets.—The tourist wishing to see real Mexican life of the average type will find it best exemplified in the streets running parallel to the river on the south side. Everything here has such a fo reign aspect that it is difficult to realize that one is within the limits of the United States. The streets are very narrow and irregular—some houses projecting much beyond the others. The houses themselves are all of adobe, one story high, and generally built around a placita, or else with a kind of a court in front. While not prepossessing outside, a glimpse through any door will reveal an interior of extreme neatness and comfort, while the flowering plants on the broad window-sills tell of the taste of those dwelling within.

15. The University of New Mexico.—In the midst of the new part of the city near the depot stands a massive and conspicuous brick structure which is the home of the first Protestant College established in New Mexico. This building is called Whitin Hall, after the family of Mr. Whitin, of Massachusetts, who were liberal benefactors of the University. The corner-stone of the Hall was laid October 21, 1882; Judge Prince being President, and Wm. M. Berger Secretary of the Trustees, and Professor H. O. Ladd, President of the Faculty.

16. The Congregational Church stands near the University, and is a neat structure of brick.

17. Church of Our Lady of Guadalupe.—This church, dedicated to the Patroness of the Mexican people, is one of the most interesting places to be visited in the city, and is made the subject of a separate description.

18. The Methodist Church is situated on the north side of the river on lower San Francisco street, and is a neat building of adobe; stuccoed.

19. The "Rosario" Chapel, or Church of Our Lady of the Rosary, is still farther west on the outskirts of the town, and is only used for funerals or on special days throughout the year. On the second Sunday after Trinity each year, an immense procession containing sometimes nearly 2,500 persons, proceeds from the Cathedral to this church carrying an image of the Virgin Mary, which is returned after twelve days. On the right side of the body of the church is a large painting of Our Lady of Guadalupe; and over the altar is a smaller picture of the Holy Family.

20. The Military Cemetery almost adjoins the Rosario Church, and contains the graves of a large number of soldiers who have died in the service in New Mexico.

21. The Military Quarter embraces all of that part of the city between the Plaza and Palace Avenue, on the south, and the State House property, on the north, except the Palace itself. The residence of the commanding officer is on Washington Avenue, and six houses for other officers occupy most of the square between Lincoln and Grant Avenues. These are generally occupied by the District Staff.

22. The Military Headquarters are at the north-west corner of the Plaza, and contain the offices of the Commanding General, the Adjutant General, Quartermaster, Commissary, Paymasters, and all the other officials of the Military District.

23. The Military Post, which is still officially called "Fort Marcy," is to the north of the officers' quarters, and extends to the Capitol Grounds. Here are the quarters of the troops which form the garrison, or are temporarily stationed here, the residences of the officers of the Post, etc. The regular "guard-mounting" every morning attracts many visitors.

24. The Presbyterian Church is a tasteful brick edifice standing on a conspicuous triangle immediately west of the Military Quarter.

25. The Capitol Square and Building.—The square immediately north of the Military Quarter was selected many years ago for the capitol of the present Territory and future State. A large and substantial building was commenced and considerable appropriations expended upon it, the work having been begun in 1859. When the Internal Revenue tax was inaugurated, about 1862, the Congressional Delegate relinquished the appropriation to complete the building, in return for temporary exemption from that species of taxation; and so the building stood in an unfinished condition for over twenty years, until the Tertio-Millennial Directors floored and roofed it, and made it very useful for the purposes of the great historic celebration of 1883.

Hardware, Queensware,

STOVES,

AND HOUSE-FURNISHING GOODS,

GUNS, PISTOLS, AMMUNITION,

———AND———

Miners' Tools, Wagon Sheets and Tents.

All kinds of Tin, Copper, and Sheet-iron work made to order. Tin Roofing a
specialty. Agents for Dupont's Powders and the Celebrated Bridge, Beach & Co.'s
Stoves, McCormick's Mowers and Reapers.

San Francisco Street,   SANTA FE, N. M.

26. The Cemetery of Odd Fellows and Masons, while belonging to these organizations, yet through their courtesy, has been used by many others for a long time. It contains monuments to many of Santa Fé's best known citizens, including a number of high government officials.

27. The Garita, or old Mexican powder magazine, is on the hill northeast of the above cemetery ; and one of the objects of historic interest that should not be overlooked. It is described in the separate sketch of Ft. Marcy, as it is on the road to that point.

28. The Old Cemetery and Chapel, on "the Loma," are likewise on that road, and have mention in that sketch. The Chapel was built about 1834.

29. The Santa Fe Academy is immediately west of the old Cemetery, and though an unpretentious building, is a successful educational establishment. The property belongs to the "Educational Association of New Mexico," but the school is temporarily under Presbyterian control.

30. The Historical Society Rooms.—These are on Washington Avenue between the Plaza and the Palace Hotel. The Historical Society is a territorial institution of recent establishment, and only obtained a "local habitation" in May, 1883. Since that time its collections have rapidly increased; and with its magnificent field of labor, it cannot fail to be a most important institution in a brief time. The rooms are open at almost all hours and strangers are always welcome. Many relics and antiquities, pictures of leading men and places in the Territory, a fine cabinet of mineral specimens, etc., will be found here.

31. The Board of Trade Rooms.—These are immediately in the rear of the Historical Rooms and connected with them. They are comfortably furnished and visitors are always welcome. Here will be found the register of visitors to the Denver Exposition of 1882; and guests are all cordially invited to leave their autographs in the same book.

32. The Bureau of Immigration.—This is an official Territorial institution, intended to afford information to visitors and prospective settlers. In its rooms can be obtained pamphlets relating to New Mexico at large, and each separate county ; and files of papers are also kept.

These thirty-two places are all easy of access and generally open to the public. Some private houses contain interesting objects and antiquities; especially those of Judge Prince and Secretary Ritch. At the former, besides a large collection of books on New Mexico, of stone implements and antique pictures, is a painting of St. Catharine executed by Zurbaran, the Spanish Painter-Royal, in 1633, at Madrid ; and at the latter, besides other rare works, will be found a copy of Lord Kingsborough's famous work on Mexican Antiquities, and of Hakluyt's Voyages.

In presenting this list of some of the places of interest in Santa Fé, as well as in the descriptions of other towns, we have purposely omitted allusion to any of the stores ; because, unless all were described, such mention would be invidious. Suffice it to say that nothing so much astonishes the average Eastern traveller as to visit one of the great wholesale houses, and see the enormous stock of goods carried and the space occupied. The filagree jewelry stores and curiosity shops always attract, the attention of tourists, as they should. No one should leave New Mexico without seeing the skillful Mexican jewellers at work with their delicate threads of gold and silver, or without buying a few souvenirs in the way of Pueblo pottery, skins, rugs, blankets, and antiquities, never omitting a piece of *amole*, or soap-root, and a package of piñons.

THE PALACE

This building, while unpretentious in its architecture and appearance, yet unquestionably possesses more historic interest than any other in the country. Its history is largely that of the town, and many points of interest connected with it have been touched upon in the sketch of historical events relating to Santa Fe. No tourist should fail to visit it, and especially to observe the extreme thickness (over five feet) of some of the old walls. No one can tell how many scenes of revelry and gaiety, or of gloom and suffering this structure has seen. Here was the reception room of the governor, and here the dungeon of the state prisoner; here expeditions were arranged, and here conspiracies were planned. For years the Captain-General was practically an autocrat; for while an appeal could be taken in some cases from his action, yet Mexico and Madrid were so distant that it was generally of little avail.

While certain parts of the building have varied in their uses, yet the portion now occupied as a Governor's residence has been so from time immemorial. Before the American occupation, the extreme west end of the building was used as a jail; next came the quarters of the regular guard; then a room devoted to the Guard of Honor of Gov. Armijo, and then came the Governor's residence and office. The room in which Governor Alencaster received Pike, in 1807, and that in which Gov. Armijo received the envoy of Kearney, in 1846, is to the east of the Governor's entrance; east of that were the various government offices, prominent among them that of the Commissary. Every room has its history, but space forbids their full enumeration here.

OLD FORT MARCY

Is situated on a high hill a short distance northeast of the Palace Hotel, and the view from the summit is the finest to be obtained in the vicinity of the city. Historically this is a place of great interest, as a moment's observation will show that it is a commanding military position, and that the army in possession of the hill controls the city. In the frequent wars between the native nations before the coming of the Spaniards, this was no doubt the scene of many a warlike encampment, and when, in 1680, the Pueblos revolted against the Spanish rule, this hill was occupied by the Indian forces under Popé, on August 11, 1680, and the city besieged for nine days, when the Spaniards were obliged to evacuate it and march towards El Paso. On the 16th of December, 1693, Vargas re-entered Santa Fé with his army and a number of families and settlers, but instead of occupying the houses they encamped for some days on the hills just north of the town, a portion of them probably being on Ft. Marcy hill. Here they stayed until the day after Christmas, when the Taños Indians, having refused to give up their quarters around the Plaza, the Spaniards made an assault on the town, and after a most desperate struggle succeeded in taking possession of it on December 27th. Through all the operations down to the final pacification, this commanding hill was a prominent position, and saw many an encampment and many a council fire.

When the American army under Gen. Kearney came in 1846, taking Santa Fe on August 18th, one of the first matters that was undertaken was the erection of a fortress to command the city. The site of Ft. Marcy was chosen, and Lieut. Gilmer, of the topographical corps, and L. A. MacLean, a member of Capt. Reid's company of Missouri Volunteers, were appointed to superintend the construction. It was built by details of volunteers who complained grievously of having to do this laborious work, when they had simply entered the army to fight. In shape it was a

PORTAL ENTRANCE TO THE SAN JUAN, ON THE LINE OF D. & R. G. R. R.

BLAIN BROS.,

Wholesale and Retail

GENERAL MERCHANDISE,

Guns, Pistols and Ammunition,

CLOTHING, BOOTS, SHOES, HATS & CAPS,

JEWELRY AND MUSICAL INSTRUMENTS,

Stationery, Books and Notions.

Constantly on hand the largest stock and assortment of fine

CHINA and GLASSWARE,

Hardware, Harness and Saddlery,

LOOKING GLASSES, PAINTINGS. CHROMOS.

to be found in the Territory.

Dealers in Second-Hand Goods.

San Francisco Street,

SANTA FE, - - NEW MEXICO.

irregular tri-decagon, large enough to accommodate a thousand troops and mount many cannon. Its walls were massively built of adobes, and it was named in honor of the then Secretary of War, Wm. L. Marcy. Behind the Fort was a block-house, the ruins of which are yet very distinct. A plan of the Fort is found in Hughes' Doniphan's Expedition, page 89. The height of the Fort above the Plaza is 291 feet.

On the way to Fort Marcy from Washington Avenue, you pass several historic spots. The adobe building with two bastions at the corners, on the first hill south of the Academy, is the old "GARITA," used for very many years by the Mexican authorities as a depository of powder for their army. The small square house near it is the Guard House used in protecting the Garita. On the west side of the Garita, close to the wall, the four leaders of the revolution of 1837—Desiderio Montoya, Antorio Abad Montoya, Gen. Chopon, and Alcalde Esquibel, were executed by command of Gen. Armijo, after sentence by court-martial, in January, 1838. They were made to kneel in a row close to the wall, and the soldiers appointed to shoot them were drawn up in a line in the road below. A little further on we come to the

THE OLD CEMETERY AND RUINED CHAPEL,

which for many years prior to the American occupation were in use by the Mexicans. The cemetery was enclosed by a substantial adobe wall, but all now in ruins.

THE NEW CATHEDRAL.

The Cathedral now being erected is by far the largest and most expensive church in the Territory. It is built in the French style of architecture, of a light brown stone, with two towers in front. Its erection was commenced in 1869, on July 24th, but was suspended at one time for nearly five years, on account of lack of funds. Archbishop of Lamy has been indefatigable in pushing on the great work to completion, and has devoted much of his private means, as well as many offerings from friends in France, to the purpose. It is being built around the

THE OLD CATHEDRAL

Of San Francisco, which was the Parish Church until Santa Fé was made the residence of a Bishop, about 1850. This old church is of adobe, and contains many objects of interest. In shape it is cruciform, like nearly all the large churches in New Mexico. The most striking object within it is the great Reredos, behind the altar, made of native stone carved in relief, which extends across the entire width of the chancel recess, and reaches to the eaves of the building. This bears two inscriptions in ovals, reading as follows:

"A devocion de Señor Don Francisco Antonio Marin del Valle, Gobernador y Capitan General de este Reino."

"Y de su esposa Maria Ygnacia Martinez de Ugarte, 1761."

It is in three sections, with carved arabesque columns between them, the whole being painted in appropriate colors. In the centre is a large, life sized statue; and above that a relief of St. James on horseback killing turbaned Saracens. Over that, crowning the whole reredos, is a representation of St. Joseph, and of the Virgin and Child.—On the north side are two carved pictures in stone relief,—of St. Anthony of Padua, with the Holy Child, and a tree; and of St. Ignacius, with a book and standard. Opposite these are St. John Nepomuceno, with cross and palm, and St. Francis Xavier baptizing Indians, the water being poured from a shell. Taken altogether, this reredos is the most extraordinary piece of sculpture in the Territory. It was originally in the church of Our Lady of Light, on the Plaza.

Opposite the chancel, and facing the altar (which is itself well worthy of notice for the beauty of its metallic workmanship) are two very large paintings, made to match each other, one being of San Francisco, and one of San Antonio de Padua. Each is surrounded by cherubs.

The chapel to the south is that of San José. In this are a number of beautiful and valuable pictures. Over the altar the large picture is St. Joseph, and underneath that, is a statuette of the same Saint, crowned, and with the Infant Christ.—On the right the upper picture is also of St. Joseph, then comes a narrow portrait of a monk, and below that one of St. Augustine wearing a bishop's mitre. On the opposite side are pictures of the Good Samaritan, of a Saint in penitential robes, and of a Franciscan Friar.

On each side of the altar is a life-size image, made of wood, one being of Our Lord crowned with thorns, the other of St. John the Apostle.

On the left is a large picture of Our Lady of Carmel aiding suffering beings in purgatory, another of the crucifixion, and modern paintings of Our Lady of Sorrows, and "Ecce Homo." Opposite are pictures of the Virgin and Child, and of the Resurrection.

On the north side is the Chapel of the Blessed Virgin, also containing many interesting works of art. On each side of the altar is a life size figure of a female saint, the one on the right in bright colors, and that on the left in black. Over the altar is an image of the Virgin clothed in rich silk vestments, above which is a picture of the Madonna, and beneath an "Ecce Homo." On the left and right are paintings of the Assumption of the Virgin and of St. Joseph, companion pieces, and between them and the altar smaller pictures representing two female saints. On the right side of the chapel, as you approach the altar, are pictures of the Virgin standing on the new moon; of the Crucifixion, St. John, the Virgin, and Mary Magdalen being at the foot of the cross; and of the Holy Family, with a representation of purgatory below. On the opposite side is a very large picture of the Holy Family.

In the body of the church are the usual "Stations of the Cross," of large size, and on the north side a niche containing an image of Christ in the Tomb, used in the ceremonies between Good Friday and Easter. Over the chancel are three stained glass windows, with figures representing St. Francis, St. Joseph, and the Immaculate Conception.

In the sacristy, is a most admirable painting of Our Lord; and a statue in wood and enamel of San Antonio de Padua, of Spanish origin, eighteen inches high, and similar in style to those at Santa Cruz and the Guadalupe Church. In the same place is a large image of the Santo Niño Conquistador.

THE CHURCH OF OUR LADY OF GUADULUPE

Is situated on the south side of the river, not very far from the railroad depot. It is massively built of adobe, cruciform in shape, and, until recently, was surmounted by a tower containing several bells made of native New Mexican copper.

For a number of years prior to 1882 this church was very little used, except on the Festival of Our Lady of Guadulupe (December 12th); but was a favorite spot for the antiquarian and the tourist, as it was full of curious and interesting paintings and other articles, some of which were of special value. But a short time ago the

THE
First National Bank
OF LAS VEGAS, N. M.

Authorized Capital,	-	-	-	-	$500,000
Paid in Capital,	-	-	-	-	100,000
Surplus Fund,	-	-	-	-	25,000

OFFICERS:

JEFFERSON REYNOLDS, President.

GEO. J. DINKEL, Vice-President.

JOSHUA S. RAYNOLDS, Cashier.

J. S. BISHOP, Assistant Cashier.

ASSOCIATE BANKS:

Central Bank, Albuquerque, New Mexico; First National Bank, El Paso, Texas.

CORRESPONDENTS.

First National Bank, New York.

First National Bank, Denver, Colo.

First National Bank, Pueblo, Colo.

Colorado National Bank, Denver, Colo.

Kansas City Banks, Kansas City, Mo.

Percha Bank, Kingston, New Mexico.

First National Bank, Chicago, Ills.

First National Gold Bank, San Francisc

First National Bank, Santa Fe, N. M.

State Savings Ass'n St. Louis, Mo.

Bank of Deming, Deming, New Mexico.

Socorro County Bank, Socorro, N. M.

Ketelsen & Degatau, Chihuahua, Mexico.

innovating spirit of the times laid its hand on this venerable edifice, and regarding present utility as more important than antique interest, cut windows through the massive walls, which bring a mid-day glare in place of the old " dim, religious light ;" replaced the flat, earthen roof with a high peaked one of shingles ; built a wooden spire of the strictest New England meeting-house pattern in the place of the venerable tower, and filled the body of the church with rows of wooden pews, covering the ancient adobe floor which had been pressed by the knees of the faithful devoutly bent in prayer for a century and a half of time. It is now used by the English-speaking Roman Catholics.

The first thing which strikes the visitor is the great thickness of the massive walls; and his attention is next attracted by the long rows of *vigas*, round and smooth, which support the roof. Each *viga* is itself supported by a timber at each end, which, in the style universal in all the older churches in the Territory, are all elaborately carved. These features fortunately could not be removed by the devastating hand of innovation, and so remain as enduring witnesses to the devotion, liberality, and skill of those who erected this edifice in honor of the great Patroness of the Mexican race.

The church contains some modern images of more than ordinary excellence, but we pass them by in order to draw attention to the paintings, etc., which give to it its special interest and importance.

Principal among these is the great painting behind the altar, which shows considerable artistic skill besides being entirely appropriate to its position in this particular church, dedicated to Nuestra Señora de Guadalupe. This altar-piece is a very large picture, or rather group of pictures, about fourteen feet high by ten feet wide. It is composed of six paintings in all, two on each side, one in the center, and one over the center. The central picture is the usual one of Our Lady of Guadalupe, which, of course, is unchangeable, as all are copies of the original which appeared on the tilma of the shepherd. Around this are four pictures representing four scenes in the story of the Virgin of Guadalupe. The first scene is on the right hand above, representing the Virgin appearing to the Shepherd, Juan Diego, and the latter hastening to obey her command. Opposite to this is the second scene, when the Shepherd returns after being repulsed by the Bishop of Mexico—three angels appearing above him. Below this, being the lower left hand picture, is represented the third scene, when Diego brings the roses in his tilma at the command of the Virgin ; and opposite this, the fourth and last scene, where on opening the tilma before the Bishop, the miraculous painting of Our Lady appears. Above the whole is a representation of the three persons of the Trinity, the Son being distinguished by the nail-marks in his hands.

The most interesting and curious single picture in this church is one on a large copper-plate, 28x18 inches, painted by Sebastian Salcedo in 1779. The frame is a unique production of art, having silver corners and a silver ornament on each of the four sides. The painting itself is made up of a number of other smaller pictures, the central one being "Our Lady of Guadalupe," surrounded by angels and patriarchs presenting crowns. Above her are seven different scenes in the history of her appearance to Diego; four of them similar to those in the great altar-picture, and three of other scenes. Below, on the left, is a portrait of Pope Benedict XIV., and on the right, an emblematic picture of the Mexican Empire, personified as a female. This picture is over the entrance to the Sacristy.

There are five paintings on canvas, all uniform in size, which, before the alterations to the church, were upon its walls, and have since been removed to the Sacristy, thus unfortunately depriving the church of its great attraction. These are all of considerable antiquity, and several of them are very curious and interesting because they reproduced the costumes of the age in which they were painted. They are as follows:

1.—Madonna and Child. In this the dress of the Virgin is in the curious style of the Seventeenth Century in Spain, reminding one in an exaggerated form of the hoop skirts of more recent days.

2.—The Holy Family. This represents the Virgin and St. Joseph visiting St. Elizabeth; the Infant Saviour and John the Baptist complete the picture.

3.—Our Lady of Guadalupe. An old copy of the celebrated Mexican picture.

4.—Madonna and Child. The peculiarity of this is the curious flowered dress of the Virgin.

5.—The Virgin Mary, alone. With clasped hands.

In the gallery is a large and curious painting, in the Mexican style, of a Saint, probably St. Francis. The figure occupies all the centre of the canvas, behind it is a large cross, and over the head are two angels holding crowns. In the lower left hand corner is another angel presenting a crown, and on the right side, opposite, a table with a skull upon it. The picture is far from artistic, and has no pretensions to beauty; but it is curious and interesting, and a type of many paintings executed in the Territory or in Northern Mexico.

The church contains two antique statuettes, which well exemplify the high art of Spain, and the crude American style of a century or two ago. The first is one of the finest specimens of wood carving, combined with enamel work, that is to be found in the country. But four others of this style are known in the Territory. The one in question represents the Virgin, standing in the crescent of the new moon, surrounded by clouds, a beautiful cherub's face being directly beneath the figure. The robes are of exquisite workmanship, representing embroidery, and the coloring is in rich red and purple, contrasted with black and gold. The statue is about fifteen inches high, and will well repay examination. The other statue is about eighteen inches high, made of wood and plaster, and represents St. Joseph. Scarcely could there be a stronger artistic contrast than between these two specimens!

This church also contains some rich embroideries, a part of which were originally clerical vestments, and a portion altar coverings.

The visitor should also be sure to see a curious cross of iron, with brass ornaments at the top and ends of the cross piece, and some old pictorial printed sheets, printed in red and black.

Excursions from Santa Fe.

These are numerous and in various directions, but can only be briefly mentioned. They can be made in a carriage, on horse-back, on burros, or the shorter ones will suit good travelers on foot. Nothing is more interesting and truly novel to most tourists, than for a party to engage the services of a number of burros and make a trip up the cañon on their backs. It is an experience never to be forgotten, and quite inexpensive.

1. Up the Canyon.—The cañon of the Santa Fé presents a series of beautiful spots, and altogether is a charming place for a ride or drive. Apart from the picturesque natural scenery, there are the water works, old mills, etc., to add variety to the scene.

2. Prospect Point is the summit of the "divide" between the Santa Fé and the Tesuque Rivers, on the railroad, about three miles north of the Plaza. The view from this elevation is magnificent and extensive.

ROYAL GORGE, ON THE LINE OF THE D. & R. G. R. R.

I. J. SHARICK,

—— : DEALER IN : ——

Watches

Clocks

Diamonds

Jewelry

The Finest Assortment & Patterns

—— OF ——

MEXICAN SILVER AND GOLD NATIVE MANUFACTURED

FILIGREE JEWELRY

IN THE TERRITORY.

3. The Pueblo of Tesuque (Tay-soo′kay).—No one should think of leaving New Mexico without visiting some of the Pueblo towns. They are the greatest objects of interest in the Territory. Here, and here only, can we see in the nineteenth century the aboriginal civilization of America, as it was presented to Cortez and the early conquerors in the sixteenth. The Pueblo of Tesuque is the nearest to Santa Fé, and consequently the most visited; but those very facts have to some extent robbed it and its inhabitants of many of the characteristics most interesting among this ancient people. It is very desirable if possible to visit some of the larger and more remote pueblos. San Juan is easily accessible on the north, and Santo Domingo is but a mile from Wallace station, while Isleta is easy to be reached from Albuquerque. But if you cannot visit any of these, then do not fail to go to Tesuque. While comparatively small, yet it has all the leading features which characterize these aboriginal towns.

4. Nambe (Nam-bay) is another Pueblo town, about eighteen miles north of Santa Fé. By devoting an entire day to the trip, both this and Tesuque can be visited. . Nambé is not a large pueblo, but is interesting because its situation is away from the ordinary line of travel, and it has consequently felt little of the influence of the modern world.

5. Agua Fria (Ah′gwah Free′ah) is a little village about five miles southwest of the city; the road being a very excellent one for driving. It contains an interesting old church which will well repay a visit. On the road is one of the points of peculiar historic interest in this vicinity being

6. The place of Assassination of Governor Perez, a little more than two miles from Santa Fé. It will be remembered that when the revolutionists rose in 1837, Governor Perez marched north to meet them, but being deserted by nearly all his men, retreated to the capital and then started south. Near the house of Don Salvador Martinez he was killed by an arrow fired by a Santo Domingo Pueblo Indian; and his assailants then forced Santiago Prada, by threats of death to cut off his head, which was carried to the rebel encampment near the Rosario Church, and treated with great indignities. The spot where Governor Perez was killed is marked by a "descanso," or heap of stones surmounted by a cross, and may be seen a little to the right of the road as one drives from Santa Fé.

7. The Cerrillos Mines.—These are 20 miles distant and are easily visited in a day. They are more fully described in connection with Cerrillos Station.

If time permits longer excursions, the hunter or fisherman will find charming localities for his favorite sport on the head waters of the Pecos, with the possibility also of becoming a millionaire by stumbling upon some great mineral discovery in this rich section.

If two or three days can be spared, in no way can it be so profitably employed as in a visit to the celebrated

Cliff Dwellings. One of the pleasantest excursions from Santa Fé is to these interesting relics of a remote antiquity. They exist in various portions of southern Rio Arriba County, some of the finest being almost directly west from Españolia and easily accessible from that point. The most convenient to Santa Fé are southwest of San Yldefonso, and the entire trip can easily be made in two days. The tourist, unless he is acquainted with the localities, should drive direct to San Yldefonso and procure a guide. He will be well repaid for the extra distance by a view of the pueblo, which is described elsewhere. The place to cross the Rio Grande is some distance below the Pueblo and near the bridge of the T., S. F. & N. R. R. From the crossing a drive of about three miles up the cañon to the west, brings us to the best camping ground, as carriages can go no further. From here we walk or proceed on horses or burros further up the same road about two miles, through very fine scenery.

A deep ravine or cañon is on the south, and on the north side an almost perpendicular wall of red rock, containing, near its summit a stratum of white limestone about twelve feet in thickness, which is everywhere indented with great holes that at first appear as if made by human beings, but are really the work of large birds. On the left of the road, about two miles above the camp, are the remains of an adobe cabin, which is a land mark for the ascent of the cliffs on the south side of the valley. This ascent is quite difficult, the latter part being up the perpendicular face of the rock, in which are cut places for the hands and feet. But the tourist is well repaid, for on the level summit of the Mesa he sees the ruins of the

Ancient Stone Pueblo of **Chippillo.**

This is of large size, being 300 feet from east to west by 320 from north to south, with entrances at the southeast and northwest corners. It is built around a plaza which contains the remains of two circular *estufas*, the sides of which are stoned; and the building itself was three rooms in width, the rooms, however, as in all pueblos, being quite small. The stones of which it was constructed was squared to about the size and shape of an adobe, and the lines of all the walls are as easily to be traced now as when this great building was occupied centuries ago. It is called by the present Pueblo Indians "Chipillo," (chip-peel'yo), and the tradition is that it was built on this *mesa*, for purposes of defense, by a people who aforetime dwelt in the valley below. The ground is covered with pieces of broken pottery, moss agate, volcanic glass, and other remains of the manufacture of arrow heads and ornaments; and altogether these ruins are as perfect a specimen of the remains of a prehistoric pueblo as exist anywhere.

To reach the Cliff Dwellings, the tourist crosses this *mesa*, and descends by steps cut in the rock on the north side. Here are found a score of the cave like habitations, deeply cut into the hard clay or limestone. All show evidences of occupation, in the blackened walls and inside rooms for the safe keeping of corn, etc. In many of the caves are rude representations of eagles, bears, horses, men, etc., and in one, the picture of a great snake or *Vipera grande*, at least twelve feet long. Crossing another valley, we reach *Cuesta Blanca*, (Quay'stah Blan'kah), where are numerous cliff dwellings, and on the top of the *mesa* the ruins of three ancient stone pueblos, and a little farther to the southwest the ruined pueblos of Pajarito, (Pah hah-ree'to), surrounded on the steep edges of the cliff with multitudes of the same cave-like habitations.

Considering the great interest now evinced in the ancient people who inhabited these towns, no trip of equal length presents as much matter of historic interest, and affords as much food for thought, as this.

Towns on the Line of the A. T. & S. F. R. R.

The tourist who comes into New Mexico from the East usually is a passenger on the Atchison, Topeka & Santa Fé Railroad, and the first sight that he has of the Territory is as he emerges from the Raton tunnel. At the risk of trenching a little on the domain of Colorado, let us beg every traveller to be on the lookout for the celebrated view of the Spanish Peaks from a point just north of the tunnel. As you ascend from Trinidad through the Devil's Cañon, on a grade of 185 feet, suddenly from the rear platform, through a vista of mountain scenery, you have for a few moments this beautiful view of the snow-clad peaks nearly 100 miles away. It is too good to be lost.

MARTIN ZIMMERMAN,   C. H. GILDERSLEEVE,   JOHN H. KNAEBEL,
President.   Vice-Pres't and Treas.   Secretary

SAN MARCIAL LAND AND IMPROVEMENT CO.

TOWN LOTS AND FARMS

FOR SALE AT

San Marcial, Socorro County, N. M.

Beautifully located on the Rio Grande River at ends of divisions of the Atchison, Topeka & Santa Fe R. R., where their extensive shops will be erected.

Surrounded by elegant agricultural land. Adapted to grapes, fruit, and grain of all kinds.

General office, Santa Fe, N. M.

Local office, San Marcial, N. M., in charge of Jay Sedgwick, Agent.

Letters of inquiry will receive prompt attention.

EDWARD HENRY,
Real Estate and Insurance Agent,
NOTARY PUBLIC AND ADJUSTER,

SIXTH STREET, NEAR ST. NICHOLAS HOTEL, LAS VEGAS, NEW MEXICO,

Represents the Oldest, the Largest and the Best Insurance Companies in the World.

SECURITY THAT SECURES.

INSURANCE THAT INSURES.

ORG'D.	NAME OF COMPANY.	LOCATION.	ASSETS.
1843	Mutual Life Insurance Company	New York City	$97,961,317 72
1863	Travelers Life & Accident Insurance Company	Hartford, Conn	6,114,502 70
1819	Ætna	Hartford, Conn	8,912,655 58
1809	North British and Mercantile	London, Eng	9,294,989 21
1853	Home	New York City	7,208,489 07
1824	Scottish Union and National	Edinburgh, Scotland	33,031,045 17
1854	Phoenix	Hartford, Conn	4,336,208 31
1836	Liverpool, London and Globe	London, Eng	31,665,194 05
1794	Insurance Company of North America	Philadelphia, Penn	8,881,053 06
1879	Lion Fire Insurance Company	London, Eng	1,340,411 11
1825	Pennsylvania Fire	Philadelphia, Penn	2,301,945 27
1849	Springfield Fire and Marine	Springfield, Mass	2,395,288 58
1861	Commercial Union Assurance Company	London, Eng	9,698,571 24
1853	American Central	St. Louis, Mo	1,188,863 73
1877	Fire Insurance Association	London, Eng	1,331,782 01

PROTECTION THAT PROTECTS.

ANCHORS THAT HOLD.

The Raton Tunnel is 7,688 feet high, and at that elevation you emerge into the pure air and see the Italian sky of New Mexico.

Raton is the first town reached, and is situated at the southerly base of the mountains. It is an active, bustling, business town of 2,500 inhabitants, whose rapid increase has come from the railroad shops and the adjacent coal mines. It was not thought of until 1880, but now is one of the most enterprising places in the Territory, and has a future which will rival many eastern railroad towns. The coal mines are principally about five miles distant at

Blossburg, which has a branch railroad running to it. The coal obtained here is bituminous, of superior quality, and inexhaustible in amount. Iron mines are also in this vicinity, and with the development of these industries the prosperity of these towns will be assured.

The road now goes almost directly south, across Colfax County, and directly through the celebrated Maxwell Grant. This great tract of land was given by the last Mexican Governor, Armijo, to Messrs. Beaubien and Miranda, about forty years ago, and contains over 1,800,000 acres; part of its area being in Colorado. It extends from the summit of the Rocky Mountains to a line considerably east of the railroad, a distance of over fifty miles, constituting a principality of itself. The next town of importance is

Springer, forty-one miles south of Raton and 716 miles from Kansas City. This is the county-seat of Colfax County, and a model Court-house of brick, with a jail of steel cells adjoining, can be seen distinctly from the cars. Few towns are more flourishing than this. It is the depot for a vast grazing and stock country to the east, extending into Texas and the Indian Territory, and it controls the trade of a large section on the west. Telephone lines connect it with the principal ranches of the county. It has an excellent public school, the people having erected a school house when there was but three dwellings in town. About a mile distant are the *Cement Works*, at which an article is being manufactured of very superior quality. From here stages run to

Cimarron, distant twenty-two miles. This was founded by the English Company which at one time owned the Maxwell Grant, as the capital of their domain; the residence of Maxwell, where he had lived like a feudal chief and dispensed feudal hospitality, being its neuclus. For many years, until 1882, it was the county-seat, and is still the headquarters of the Maxwell Land and Grant Company and the Maxwell Cattle Company. From Cimarron the road through a pass in the Rocky Mountains to Taos, ascends toward the west through a most beautiful and picturesque cañon, and is well worth a visit. This road leads to

Elizabethtown, Ute Creek, and other gold regions. The first discovery was made here in Wilson Gulch, September 22, 1866, and soon miners flocked to the locality, until Elizabethtown contained 5,000 people. In 1868 the "Big Dutch," forty-four miles long, was constructed at a cost of $300,000 to bring water from the head of Red River. This region abounds with gold, both "in place," as at the Aztec mine, and in gravel or *placers*. Being on the Maxwell Grant, the long litigations regarding that property have discouraged enterprise; but thousands can be supported here when proper arrangements are made with prospectors and miners. This is one of the best ways of reaching Taos, but we will describe that town in another place. Returning to the railroad, the next place of interest is

Wagon Mound. This was a famous point in the days of the "Trail," the mountain close to the railroad on the east being a land mark for all the travelers of the plains, and obtaining its name from its resemblance in form to a wagon and horses when seen from a distance. The curious elevations on the west side of the track are called the Santa Clara Hills. Twenty-five miles further on we come to

Watrous, but for some time before the eye has been charmed by the sight of beautiful bright green fields in a delightful valley. No more inviting prospect could be imagined, especially for the traveler who has been crossing the brown and monotonous plains. Watrous marks what was the extreme limit of settlement under the Mexican government. James Bonney had settled there in 1842 and the military reports of Emory, Abert, etc., mention that his house was the first seen for 775 miles on the march of General Kearney's army from the Missouri in 1846. Barclay's Fort was in this vicinity, having been built for protection against the Indians. The place was then called La Junta (Lah Hoontah), meaning *the junction*, because the Mora and Sapelló rivers meet here. Its name was changed to Watrous in honor of Mr. Samuel B. Watrous, who came to the Territory in 1835 lived for some time at the "Placers" and then moved here, where he has since resided. Watrous is an enterprising village, having an excellent school-house, built by subscription. From here the various points in the Mora Valley can be reached with ease.

Mora, the county seat, is about twenty-six miles distant, and is situated in a most charming valley, surrounded on all sides by high mountains. This was the later residence of Col. Ceran St. Vrain, who built the large stone mill which is a prominent feature of the village, and whose grave is conspicuous on the hill south of the town. At Mora is a college of the Christian Brothers, and a girl's academy under the Sisters of Loreto. The whole country in this vicinity is of great beauty and the valleys exceedingly fertile. The drive to Agua Negra (Ah'gwah Na'grah) is a most charming one. Near Ocaté (O-kat-ay') is the crater of a great pre-historic volcano. La Cueva (Lah Kway'vah) is a beautiful domain, formerly the property of Don Vicente Romero, and includes several fine lakes. A drive around Mora county occupying two or three days, will well repay the tourist.

Fort Union is but a short distance from Watrous. This has for many years been the principal military post in Northeastern New Mexico, and for a long time was the great store-house for the army in this section of the country. Three or four companies and a band are usually stationed here.

LAS VEGAS. (Las Vay-gass.)

Proceeding on the railroad, a ride of an hour brings us to the city of Las Vegas, the county seat of San Miguel county, and by far the largest place in New Mexico east of the mountains. It is a very important business point and whether viewed in the light of its present prosperity or its future prospects is second to no town in the Territory. But to the tourist it does not present specially great attractions. It is comparatively new, its founder having been Don Miguel Romero, who first came here in 1833, but did not permanently settle till 1840. He was the father of Trinidad, Eugenio, Hilario, Benito and Margarito Romero. The grant of the land, from the Mexican Government, was made in 1835, when twenty-nine persons were put in possession of moderate tracts, the remainder of the grant being reserved for all those inhabitants who in the future might be destitute of land. The first American to settle here was Levi J. Keithley, in 1339. He was elected a member of the first Territorial Legislature in 1847. The town grew up around the plaza, until, in 1850, all four sides were well filled. The first railroad train arrived July 4th, 1879, and at that time there was but one house on the side of the river where the depot is situated, and where the "New Town" sprung up immediately after as if by magic. The first place for the tourist to visit is the

Roman Catholic Church. This is not very old, but it is a very large edifice, built of the red sandstone which abounds in the vicinity; the form being a parallelogram with half octagonal wings on the sides for the side altars, and two towers in front. It does not possess any old paintings or sculpture, but on high festival days, with its multitude of lights, the church presents a very brilliant appearance.

The Plaza, until 1881, was an open square, generally filled with ox teams, wagons and burros. It was the center of trade for the whole county. It is now fenced in an oval form, and planted with trees and grass, making a striking contrast to its old condition of heat and dust. The most interesting spot, historically, is the

Place of Taking the Oath. Las Vegas was the first town reached by the American "Army of the West" under General Kearney, on their invasion of New Mexico in 1846. The army arrived on August 14th, and General Kearney speedily summoned the Alcalde, named Juan de Dios Maes, who was the principal local official, and with him, the Parish Priest, and some staff officers, went to the flat roof of a house on the north side of the Plaza, about the middle of the block, in order to address the people who thronged the Plaza. All was confusion and fear, for the people knew little of Americans, except as represented by the rough men of the border, and many stories had been circulated of a character to excite anxiety. The General informed them that he had not come as an enemy but a friend; that they would not in any way be molested in person or property; that no man's religion would be interfered with; and that the only change was that they were citizens of the United States, instead of Mexican subjects. He then called on the Alcalde, as the representative of the people, to take the oath of allegiance; and this was solemnly done in the sight of the great concourse before them. It is certainly an interesting historical spot where the first New Mexican took this oath of allegiance to the Great Republic, and should be visited by all strangers. It is gratifying to know that the oath in this case was much more than lip-service. For when the "Taos Insurrection" took place and Governor Bent and other officials were killed at Taos, and Mr. Waldo and his seven companions murdered at Mora, the programme was to have a general rising throughout the Territory, and a swift message was sent to the Alcalde urging such action at Las Vegas and the immediate destruction of all Americans. But the honest old man, loyal to his obligation, called a meeting of the people, which was held near the south-west corner of the Plaza, and there told them the news and then added : "You all saw me take the oath of allegiance on yonder house-top. When I did so I took it officially for you all. You are all bound as well as I, and for myself, I assure you, that I intend to live and die by that oath." The busy hum of trade is now heard on the spots where these events occurred, but they are no less interesting on that account.

The Las Vegas College, or, as it is generally called, "the Jesuit College," is the largest institution of learning in the Territory, and increases in extent and usefulness every year. It was opened in 1877, and then only consisted of one long building; subsequently two large wings were added, and when entirely completed it will be one of the most imposing structures in the south-west. It is conducted by the Fathers of the Society of Jesus, and the course of instruction is very complete.

The Sisters' Academy is in charge of the Sisters' of Loreto, and is a very useful and creditable institution.

The Academy is the handsome brick edifice on Douglas avenue in the "New Town," and the

Southern Methodist School is the large square brick building on the hill. Both are flourishing schools.

While Las Vegas, on account of its comparatively recent settlement, does not possess the objects of interest to the tourist seen in the older towns, yet it is quite fully compensated by having in its immediate vicinity the celebrated

LAS VEGAS SPRINGS.

These are situated about six miles from Las Vegas, in a beautiful cañon, through which flows the Gallinas (Gal-yee-nas) river. The virtues of these healing waters have been known for years, and long before they were thought of as a watering place the Mexicans used to come long distances to have the benefit of their curative properties. There are nearly forty of these springs in all, of which over twenty have been thoroughly analyzed. Their temperature ranges from 70° to 136°, and their chemical constituents vary almost as much as their degrees of heat. It seems marvelous that within so small an area such a variety should exist. But in this very fact consists their special and exceptional value.

For many years there had been a small hotel at the Springs, but in 1879 the "Hot Springs Hotel," a three-story granite building was erected, and soon after the foundations were laid of the sumptuous "Montezuma." Simultaneously with these improvements, the bath houses, which contain every modern appliance, are 200 feet long by 45 wide, built of red granite, and two stories high, were being constructed, and now constitute an establishment which, for perfection of appointments and variety of medicinal effects, is not equalled in the world.

It is not necessary to describe the beauty of the grounds or the natural surroundings at the Springs, for every tourist will see them. Suffice it that for comfort and elegance no watering-place in the land excels the Las Vegas Springs.

The Pecos Valley is reached by conveyance from Las Vegas, and embraces one of the most fertile and beautiful sections of the territory, especially abounding in fruit. Santa Rosa and Puerto de Luna, are two of the most important points here, and lower down is admirable grazing and farming land. Proceeding on the railroad four miles from Las Vegas is

Romero, so called after Don Trinidad Romero, late delegate in congress, whose elegant residence and ranche are conspicuous from the cars.

The Bernal Peak is a conspicuous object for fifty miles after leaving Las Vegas, from its peculiar shape. It is also called Starvation Peak, from a legend that a number of Spaniards who took refuge there were surrounded by Indian enemies until they perished from starvation. This story is not well authenticated, and occasionally the parties are transposed and the beleaguered company are Indians surrounded by Spaniards. The tourist may take his choice; but at all events he will be sure to admire the bold scenery connected with the mountain.

The railroad here makes a great semi-circle around the southern extremity of the Rocky Mountain range, and we are rapidly ascending to the highest point on the route, at the "Glorieta Divide," where the altitude is 7537 feet. The scenery all through this section is very fine, and the traveler should specially notice the wonderfully ingenius and extensive works which the railroad company have constructed along the track for miles to prevent wash-outs and other injuries from sudden floods. In the Apache Cañon, scarcely wide enough for the track, and with high perpendicular walls, the water has been known to rise forty feet in an hour. In wild and picturesque beauty few places exceed this cañon.

Before reaching Glorieta, and while ascending the heavy grade, the tourist who cannot afford a day's time to visit the locality at leisure, must not fail to observe the celebrated

TOLTEC TUNNEL, ON THE LINE OF THE D. & R. G. R. R.

J. J. FITZGERRELL,

The Live Real Estate Man

NOTARY PUBLIC,

AND COLLECTING AGENT,

LAS VEGAS, NEW MEXICO.

REFERENCES :

Maj. Gen. John A. Logan, U. S. Senator.
Hon. Philetus Sawyer, U. S. Senator.
Hon. David H. Jerome, Governor of Michigan.
Hon. L. H. Roots, Banker, Little Rock, Ark.
Hon. N. H. Thistlewood, Mayor of Cairo, Ills.
Evans, Willbank & Co., Bankers, Mt. Vernon, Ills., as well as
   other leading citizens of that city.
Col. A. W. Rodgers, Warrensburg, Mo.
Hon. Ezra Rust, Lumberman, Saginaw, Mich.

This city is the business center, the Chicago of New Mexico, the Great Health Sanitarium of the world. There have been more houses built, and more money spent for general improvements in this city than any other place in the Territory. The city offers special inducements to merchants, capitalists, mechanics, laborers, etc. Real estate and business investments pay from 25 to 200 per cent here. Come and look at our improvements—water works, street cars, gas works, telephone exchange, foundry and machine shop, colleges, academy, female seminary, mammoth business houses, doing a business extending into millions of dollars annually, and above all, our live business men. The city is now connected by rail with the famous Las Vegas Hot Springs. *Come and be convinced.* Call and see me when in the city —the latch string hangs out; will serve you with pleasure.

J. J. FITZGERRELL,

Correspondence Solicited   *The Live Real Estate Agent.*

Send for Fitzgerrell's Guide to New Mexico, for general information. *Free to all*

Ruins of Pecos, in a hill a short distance north of the track. This Pueblo was the only one east of the mountains, and for centuries stood like a sentry of civilization on the border of the wild tribes that roamed over the plains. The extent of the ruins attest what history tells of the power and population of this great pueblo. No place in America is full of more romantic traditions than Pecos. Here, it is said Montezuma was born, and from here started on the migration of the Aztec people to Mexico. Others say that here he remained until he disappeared from earth, after promising that at the end of many days he would reappear from the east in the morning light, and bidding the priests carefully preserve the sacred fire ever burning until his return. Others, again, say that he planted a tree, and then foretold the sorrows and **subjection of** his people, but assured them that one day there should come from the east an army of pale-faced men who would bring peace and prosperity with them; and that that tree should stand till all this was fulfilled; .and those believers in this last tradition assure us that the tree fell with a loud crash on the day that the Americans entered Santa Fé.

However these traditions may be, the ruins are of great enduring interest; for they show us the remains of a large city, principally built of stone, covering a great extent of land; and the ruins of the church, though rapidly disappearing before the ravages of time and the more ruthless hand of the "curiosity fiend," still are a monument to the zeal of the old Franciscan monks, and to the "faith shown by works" of the industrious people who erected it.

This Pueblo was deserted about 1840, the people having become greatly reduced in numbers by successive visitations of small-pox and other diseases. They never ceased to guard the sacred fire, and finally when they migrated to the kindred pueblo of Jemez, they carried it with them, unextinguished, to their new home.

The Glorieta Battlefield is plainly visible from the cars as they pass; and while this battle is not well known to Eastern people, it was really one of the decisive conflicts of the war of the Rebellion; for as far as this point the Southern army had marched triumphantly. They had taken Santa Fé and their government was in operation there. Nearly the whole Territory was under their control, and they were marching to seize the stores and munitions at Ft. Union. Here, at Glorieta, after a whole day of battle they were turned back. They evacuated Santa Fé and retreated southerly, never to return. But had the result been different they might have marched on, penetrating Colorado, cutting off communication with the Pacific, and so doing incalculable injury. To Col. Slough and his Colorado troops are due great credit for that good day's work; and it is likewise never to be forgotten that in the country's hour of need, New Mexico stood as loyal as Massachusetts, and her sons went into the army to an extent scarcely equalled elsewhere.

Lamy is sixty-five miles from Las Vegas; and here the branch road for Santa Fé leaves the main track. It is named after Arch-bishop Lamy.

Cerrillos (sare-reel' yoce) is the next place of importance. A smelter is located here. This town has most extraordinarily rich surroundings. Three miles to the north are the celebrated Cerrillos mines. A short distance up the Galisteo are extensive fields of placer gold. In almost every direction, or. the south, are vast fields of bituminous coal of unusual excellence, and what is most extraordinary, there are also large deposits of anthracite of superior quality in the immediate vicinity. While the town is not large now, yet with its situation on the Galisteo, and its wonderful surroundings, no place in the Territory has a more certain future.

Cerrillos Mines. These are within walking distance from Cerrillos Station, and about twenty miles from Santa Fé. The most famous of them is the "Old Turquoise Mine." This was worked by the Pueblos from time immemorial. When Cabeza de Vaca passed through, in 1537, he saw many of the stones. When

Marcos de Niza made his exploration, in 1540, he reported that they **were the principal** ornaments at Cibola and beyond; and his description of them had **much to do with bringing the Expedition of Coronado.** During the Spanish **control, before 1680, this mine was worked to an immense extent.** The turquoises for **the Spanish crown came from here.** **More than a third of the entire Chalchiutl** Mountain was **mined away.** **Besides this, there were** numerous silver mines **in** operation then. **Many old shafts are found here now.** **The** *Mina del Tiro* **has** been re-opened **to the water level.** **Of course all these mines were** closed during the Pueblo Revolution of **1680; but their locations are very observable.** This is one of the best **mineral localities in the** Territory. **The mines are generally of argentiferous galena, but gold and copper are** also found. **The common name of the village** in the mining district **is Carbonateville, but its post-office name is Turquesa, (Toor-kay'sah).** A mile to the north is Bonanza City, where the Marshal Bonanza Mine, and the Gonzalez Reduction Works are.

Wallace is the next important town, it is the first point **from which the Rio** Grande is visible. **Most travellers know it as a meal station; but it has worthier reasons for** being remembered. **It is** the only **turquoise market in the country.** **The cars are surrounded by a host of** Pueblo Indians **from Santo Domingo who come to sell turquoise.** **It is always** green and the most of it is **imperfect; but occasionally with care you can find** an excellent piece of good clear **color.** **Within sight from here is the**

Pueblo of Santo Domingo, and every real tourist ought to stop here for a day, so as to see it. It is an extensive pueblo, **and has** the advantage of show-ing two styles of architecture, the ancient and the modern, as half of the town was washed away some years ago by the Rio Grande, and those unfortunate enough to be left homeless rebuilt on the east side **of the town.** The older houses are entered in regular Pueblo style, from the roof, **but the new** ones **have doors, the** reason of the old style, for purposes of defense, having disappeared **now.** **For the** tourist who does not wish to go far from a railroad, this presents the best opportunity to visit **an important** and characteristic pueblo, and should not be missed. **The old church** here **is of much interest.** The doors have various carvings upon them, including **the Spanish coat-of-arms.** **The** image of St. Dominick, (Santo Domingo), for whom the **pueblo is named, is nearly** life-size; **and on the annual festival day,** (August 4th), is taken from the chapel, **and carried in** the procession to **a temporary** building made of branches of trees, **and elaborately ornamented,** and **there remains during** all the **ceremonial dances etc.** **This festival lasts all day,** and is very interesting. No one who can arrange to **be present at that time should** lose **the opportunity.** **At this point we enter the**

Rio Grande Valley. **Nothing could be more beautiful or more fertile.** **Grain,** vegetables, **and fruit all grow luxuriantly.** **The size of the onions, beets,** cabbages, **and** other vegetables produced, is extraordinary. **Vineyards abound on** every side, **and are found** now all the **way to El Paso.** Peaches, apricots, plums, pears, apples, etc., all do well. **While a large** part of the valley is devoted to ordinary grains, **it** may be assumed without doubt that in ten years, it will be one great **orchard and** vineyard from end to end, supplying with its luscious products the great **north-western** section between the Mississippi and the Rocky Mountains.

Various pretty villages are passed as the **train** moves on, among them Algodones **(Al-go-do′ness),** and Alameda (Al-ah-may′dah), **which** are **Mexican towns, and San** Felipe **(Fay-lee′pay),** and Sandia (San-dee′ah), **which are pueblos.** **The first town of** special importance is

Bernalillo, (Bair-nah-leel′yo), **which was** long **the** county **seat of the county** of the same name, until 1883, and is **the** wealthiest **and most** aristocratic **town in the**

R. C. HEISE,

CHAS. ETHERIDGE,

Notary Public,

valley It is the residence of the Perea family, who own a half a million of sheep, of Don Mariano S. Otero, late Delegate, etc.   It is a charming spot, embowered in vineyards and orchards, and thus has been saved from the desecration of the common grocery and the saloon. Its church is an interesting one, containing a number of objects of value, and will well repay a visit.   The Christian Brothers and the Sisters of Loreto both have schools here. From this point stages run to the

Jemez Springs, (Hay'mess), situated 35 miles north-west.   Apart from the curative properties of the waters here, the situation is peculiarly charming. No more beautiful scenery is to be found anywhere than in the vicinity of Jemez. A large and interesting Pueblo town is near at hand, and not far distant are the celebrated ruins of the Old Pueblo. Every foot here is full of historic interest.   In this little valley, not far from Zia (See'ah) and Santa Ana, Coronado and his successors in travel found the largest of the Pueblo cities. From the earliest records Jemez itself was a place of importance. Here Espejo came in 1583 ; here the priest, Juan de Jesus, was cruelly killed in 1680 ; here Vargas held his conferences with the native authorities in 1692. To write the whole history would require a volume. But no one has thoroughly seen New Mexico who has not been to Jemez.

The Old Placers, (Plah-sair's) **New Placers, &c.,** are reached either from Bernalillo or from Wallace. The Old Placers were first discovered in 1828, by a herder from Sonora, who found particles of gold in the sand ; and quickly attracted a crowd of fortune-seekers.   The washing was done by hand or in small "rockers," water being very scarce and the greater part of the work being done in the winter, when melted snow was used. From $60,000 to $80,000 a year was thus extracted.   The principal village of the region was called Dolores. In 1839 the "New Placers" were discovered a short distance to the south-west, and the miners soon crowded to the new Eldorado. The village of Tuerto quickly grew into a bustling town, and in 1845 contained no less than twenty-two stores. For several years the product of this entire region was about $250,000 annually ; but the limit to the crude, hand-working processes employed was finally reached, and the vast stores of golden dust beneath the surface now awaits the development for which capital to bring a full supply of water is required. The "Old Copper Mine" at San Pedro is now being extensively worked ; and, besides its great value, produces the most beautiful cabinet specimens of rich colors that can be imagined.

Golden is a new mining town which has taken the place of Tuerto, and in the future bids fair to be one of the most prosperous mining centers in New Mexico.

ALBUQUERQUE.

Fifteen miles below Bernalillo and 918 from Kansas City, on the east bank of the Rio Grande, stands Albuquerque (Al-boo-kair'kay), named in honor of the Duke of Albuquerque, who was Governor and Captain-General of New Mexico in 1705. It is the county seat of Bernalillo county, and one of the most flourishing cities of the South-west. The old town is situated directly on the Rio Grande, but when the railroad was constructed it was unfortunately placed so far to the east as to cause the building of a separate town, often called New Albuquerque. The growth and prosperity of this new town have been phenomenal, fine blocks of substantial buildings attesting to the enterprise and business success of the citizens. While the "new town" will attract the merchant, the tourist will be drawn to Old Albuquerque, with its groves of fruit-trees, its beautiful vineyards, and its spacious adobe houses, telling of the generous hospitality of those who dwell therein. The great church on the Plaza will first attract attention; but the lover of art and antiquities will be disappointed to find that it contains little of historic or artistic interest. The records here extend back to 1743, but the church building itself is comparatively modern. Adjoining it is a college in charge of the Jesuit Fathers, who have their head-quarters in the Territory here. There is also a Sisters' School. The Albuquerque Academy was founded in 1879, moved to the new town in 1882, and is a very flourishing institution, with over 150 scholars. Almost all churches and denominations are represented here by religious edifices of solidity, taste, and beauty. The Territorial Fair is held here each fall, permanent fair-grounds having been arranged, including exhibition-buildings, race-track, etc. The display of fruit and vegetables, the product of the valley, is surpassed nowhere in the country. The attention of the tourist is called to the fact, which otherwise might escape his observation, that the great majority of the buildings here, which, apparently are constructed of ordinary adobes, that is of sun-dried, moulded bricks, are in reality built of blocks of a peculiar turf, full of interlacing roots, cut of the proper size, and then sun-dried. These are used in many places in the valley in place of moulded adobes, and are by some thought to be even more durable.

Albuquerque has always been celebrated for the beauty of its ladies, and even a short visit will prove to the observer that it has not deteriorated in that respect. Oddly enough, two books written forty years apart, by persons both of whom saw the city as virtual prisoners, bear witness to this singular beauty of the girls of this city. Kendall, in his "Santa Fé Expedition," in describing the privations and cruelties incident to the march to himself and the other prisoners from San Miguel to El Paso, stops to pay a glowing tribute to the beauty of a girl who was watching the prisoners pass, from an adobe wall in Albuquerque; and Lieutenant Pike, in his account of his enforced march to Chihuahua, speaks of a dinner which he enjoyed in this city through the hospitality of a leading citizen, and adds "and to crown all, we were waited on by half a dozen of those beautiful girls, who like, Hebe at the feast of the gods, converted our wine into nectar, and with their ambrosial breath shed incense on our cups"! Surely if captives can be so enthusiastic, there must be reason for admiration.

The Atlantic & Pacific Railroad makes its connection with the A., T. & S. F. at Albuquerque, and has here its offices, shops, etc., which form quite a village of themselves. That railroad, with its towns and scenic attractions, will be spoken of hereafter.

Proceeding on our route southerly, we next come to

Isleta, (Eace-late'ah), about ten miles distant. This is an Indian Pueblo, the most southerly of any, and one of the most interesting. The language spoken here is entirely different from that of most of the pueblos in this vicinity, but is identical with that of Taos, which is the most northerly pueblo. This strange distribution of the Pueblo languages has never been explained. Ten miles further on we come to

Los Lunas (Loce Loo'nass), the county seat of Valencia. This is a purely Mexican town, and has long been the residence of the Luna family, for whom it is named. Great quantities of sheep are owned here, but they are kept on ranches at a distance. Proceeding still another ten miles we arrive at

Belen (Bay-lain'), another typical Mexican town; and the residence of one important branch of the Chavez family. The whole Rio Grande valley for many miles along here is one continuous line of vineyards, orchards, and fields of grain, the houses being so close as to constitute almost an unbroken village. Many leading families reside here, nearly all being large sheep-owners. The next place of special

WHOLESALE GROCERS,

ALBUQUERQUE, N. M.

A LARGE AND COMPLETE LINE OF

Staple and Fancy Groceries.

Provisions, Flour and Feed.

AGENTS FOR THE CELEBRATED

SCHUTTLER WAGONS

——— AND ———

DIAMOND CREAMERY BUTTER.

Socorro (So-core′ro). This is a city, and the county seat of Socorro County. The old town is situated on a beautiful piece of slightly elevated land, half a mile from the river. The town was named for Our Lady of Succor, and was one of the early Spanish settlements. At that time there was a number of Pueblo towns in the vicinity, the largest being at Senecu, a short distance south. During the Pueblo revolution of 1680, Socorro was entirely destroyed, and when Vargas crossed the river to visit the town in 1692, he found everything, including the old church, completely in ruins. He paid a visit to the warm spring at the foot of the mountain, and then continued on his journey toward Santa Fé.

Socorro has a future in prospect not surpassed by any city in the Territory. It is literally surrounded by mining camps of exceptional richness; and it is situated in the center of a splendid agricultural and horticultural region of the valley. For a place of residence it has no equal on the Rio Grande. Local causes, unnecessary to recall, for some time held it back; but its day of prosperity is sure to come. The tourist who takes an interest in such things will have a fine opportunity to examine both a Stamp Mill and Smelting Works but a short walk from the town. The mountain views here are beautiful, and charming drives can be had in half-concealed cañons shaded by evergreens and varieties of the poplar. The church is, as usual, the principal place to visit; but while large, it is not very old. The zealous antiquarian will find much of interest, however, by examining the foundations of the original church, which are plainly recognizable just behind the present edifice, and which were deprived of their upper structure over two centuries ago. The great spring which Vargas journeyed to see in 1692, should certainly be visited. It is quite warm, and the volume of water surprisingly large. The zealous Sisters of Loreto have one of their schools here, and always courteously receive visitors. Professor Longuemare, if in town, should be seen, as he has a fine collection of New Mexican antiquities which he is always ready to show to those who appreciate such treasures.

Socorro is the starting point for so many surrounding towns and mining camps that it is difficult to enumerate them. Among the most important, however, are White Oaks, the Madalenas, the Oscuras, the Black Range, and the Mogollons. Twenty miles below Socorro we pass the battle-field of

Valverde, one of the battles of the Rebellion commemorated on the monument at Santa Fé; and seven miles more bring us to

San Marcial, where a flourishing town is growing up around the depot, while the quaint old Mexican town of that name is about a mile distant. This is the point from which Fort Craig, a well-known U. S. military post, is reached. A little south of San Marcial the railroad crosses to the east side of the Rio Grande, and then leaving the river, passes along the celebrated

Jornada del Muerto, or "Journey of Death," an extensive desert without water, which was the terror of the early travellers.

Engle is a station sixty-five miles south of Socorro, from which stages run to the Black Range; and it is also the starting point to the San Andres Mining District.

The Black Range district is one of the richest in New Mexico, both in mines and in beautiful, well-watered spots for ranches and orchards. Until recently it was mostly included in the "Hot Springs Indian Reservation," and after that was taken from the Indians, they continued to return to the beautiful country which they loved, and many bloody scenes occurred in the early settlement. This retarded settlement.

Fairview, Chloride, Robinson, and Grafton are the principal towns in the Black Range, Fairview being the first reached, near the Cuchilla Negra (Coo-cheel′yah Nay′grah) Mountains, and Chloride, a well-laid-out and beautifully situated town, at the mouth of Chloride Gulch. The stage passes through the Mexican town of Cuchilla Negra, which is of considerable size and surrounded by green fields and rich pastures.

Rincon (Reen-con'e), meaning a "corner," is the point of junction of the line of railroad proceeding south to El Paso and that which goes westerly to Deming.

Continuing our journey on the former, we follow the course of the Rio Grande into the rich and beautiful

Mesilla Valley. This is perhaps the most fertile tract in the Territory—in fact nothing anywhere can excel it—and its southern situation, as well as low altitude, makes its season full a month in advance of the northern parts of New Mexico. A considerable portion of this valley was not included in the original boundaries of the Territory, but was afterwards acquired by the United States as part of the "Gadsden Purchase." Grapes of all kinds flourish here; fine fig trees may be seen in full bearing; and almost every kind of fruit abounds. To the east are the Organ Mountains, whose sharp peaks present an appearance different from almost any other range, and apart from their mineral richness, add materially to the beauty of the landscape. The principal town of the valley is

Las Cruces, (The Crosses) which is now the county seat of Doña Ana County, the Legislature having passed an act removing it to this point, in 1882. The Court house is situated about half way between the old town and the railroad depot. and with the adjoining jail, cost $40,000. When entirely completed, it is expected to be the finest in New Mexico. Beautiful vineyards and orchards are on every side, and fruit of all kinds abounds from July to October. A large wholesale business is done by the merchants here, who supply retail establishments in all directions. The principal attraction to the tourist is the church, which, although not old, having been built about 1854, yet contains a number of interesting paintings removed from former edifices. The church itself is of enormous length, being no less than 215 feet from front to rear, and is built in the usual style. The principal pictures are of Spanish origin and date back about two centuries. Behind the altar are two large paintings, respectively, of Santo Domingo and Santo Rita, between them being a beautiful modern statue of St. Genevieve. Statues of the Virgin and St. Joseph of similar style are in the body of the church. In the sacristy are old paintings of St James and St. John Baptist, and also of a female saint, bearing the palm and the chains as emblems of her martyrdom. On the other side is a good example of Mexican art in a picture of Nuestra Stuora del Refugio. The *Ostensorium* should not be overlooked, as it is very large, elaborately made of silver heavily plated with gold, and altogether superior to those usually seen.

At the south end of the main street stands the Academy of the Visitation, an excellent school, in charge of the Sisters of Loreto, where about two hundred pupils are annually educated. The public school is one of the best in the Territory and well worthy a visit.

Mesilla (Mes-seel'yah) is a beautiful village about three miles south-west from Las Cruces. It is embowered in vineyards and orchards, and its gardens are visions of beauty in the summer. For many years it was the county seat of Doña Ana County, and the seat of a land-office, but both of these advantages were lost in 1882 and 1883. No tourist should fail to visit the vineyard of T. J. Bull, Esq., which is one of the largest and most successful in the Territory. On one side of the plaza stands the parish church, which does not possess any paintings, but contains four admirably executed statues in the modern French style. That behind the altar represents San Albino; to the left and right are images of Our Savior and the Virgin, and half way down the nave, on the left side, is a statue of San José. The only objects of interest to the antiquary are two large stone fonts, which will well repay

GRAND CANYON OF THE COLORADO, ON LINE OF A. & P. R. R.

LAND GRANT

—OF THE—

Atlantic and Pacific Railroad Co.,

20,000,000 Acres of Land for Sale in New Mexico and Arizona.

The Land Grant of this Company extends entirely across the Territories of New Mexico and Arizona, between the 34th and 36th degrees of north latitude, with a width of 80 miles, and comprises the best grazing lands of both Territories, and in the valleys are many desirable localities of good agricultural lands susceptible of irrigation. A sufficiency of water has been found wherever cattle and sheep have been grazed, and large herds have been grazed in the country west of Albuquerque ever since the coming of the Mexicans. Wells with good water have been successfully sunk. On the very summit of the Sierra Madre, in the vicinity of Fort Wingate, the large herds of the Navajo Indians (a tribe numbering some 12,000 or 15,000 souls) have been grazed for the last hundred years, and good crops of corn, oats, barley and garden vegetables are grown by irrigation.

A stream of running water (the Rio San Jose) rises near the summit of the Sierra Madre, and runs eastward seventy-five miles to the Rio Puerco. The company's road traverses the whole length of the valley of the San Jose. There are numerous fine valleys opening out to the valley of the San Jose, flanked by grassy and wooded hills, upon which there is an open growth of small cedar and pinon. There is an extensive belt of good pine timber on the mountains, near the railroad, and numerous large springs are found on the eastern slope of the Sierra Madre. There is a large coal field west of Fort Wingate which is fully explored, and which will soon provide labor for a large population; and there are coal deposits on the eastern slope of the Sierra Madre. Many varieties of building stone are found in great quantity along the line of the railroad.

In Arizona the grazing areas are supplied with good water, and the grazing is described by competent United States surveyors to be equal to, if not better, than that of Wyoming or Montana. The Navajo Indians grow corn each season, without irrigation, in the valley of the Puerco of the west, on the Company's land; on the line of the road, and good crops of corn, sorghum, oats, barley, and garden vegetables are grown in the valley of the Little Colorado.

There is an extensive timber belt on the San Francisco mountains, through which the line of the railroad passes, diversified by beautiful valleys and parks, with good water, and wonderful canyons.

The line of the road traverses a picturesque country, not at all monotonous, and much more inviting than were the plains of Kansas.

The road is completed and in operation to the Colorado River, 575 miles from Albuquerque, N. M., and there connects with the railroad system of California, reaching San Diego, Los Angeles, and all points on the Pacific coast to San Francisco, and shortens the distances by 300 miles.

The valley of the Rio Grande has an elevation of 5,000 feet above the sea, and the passes of the Sierra Madre, and the San Francisco mountains in Arizona, have an elevation of 7,000 feet, with a depression at Winslow, on the Little Colorado, of 5,000 feet elevation; which gives a salubrious climate of mild winters, and cool nights in summer, and insures a healthful climate and a promise of thrifty and prosperous states when the Territories shall, within a few years, be established as such.

Maps will be forwarded on application, and accredited persons desirous of inspecting grazing lands with a view to purchase and establish grazing ranches, will be given facilities for that purpose.   Address,

THOMAS A. SEDGWICK,   **JAMES A. WILLIAMSON,**
Land Agent,   Land Commissioner,
Albuquerque, N. M.   87 Milk St. Boston, Mass.

inspection. In this town there is a weekly newspaper, the *Mesilla News*, ably edited for many years by Ira M. Bond.

Originally the Rio Grande ran between Mesilla and Las Cruces, but a sudden change in the course has brought them both on the same side.

Forty-four miles from Las Cruces, and 340 from Santa Fé, is the city of

El Paso, Texas. It takes its name, as does Paso del Norte (Pass'o de Nor'tay), across the river in Mexico, from the ford in the Rio Grande at that point, which has been for centuries the crossing-place for travellers.

These places are, of course, beyond our limits, and we only venture to say that El Paso has railroad advantages which cannot fail to make it an important business center; that Paso del Norte is a quaint Mexican town, containing a large and interesting church, which should surely be visited, and where the same Padre Ortiz whose kindness Kendall and Ruxton so warmly wrote of in 1842 and 1846, officiated for forty years; and that no tourist having even two days to spare, or in fact if he has to take the time from other places, should fail to see

Chihuahua, which is a city of nearly 20,000 inhabitants, built of white stone, with which the streets are also flagged, and in true Mexican style; containing a magnificent parish church which cost over $700,000, and would require pages to describe; and whose market-place, plaza, alameda, and other churches are places of too much interest to be neglected or passed unobserved. Besides all which, Chihuahua is the cleanest and the best policed city on the continent.

From El Paso the Mexican Central Railroad proceeds directly south toward the City of Mexico, the Southern Pacific runs north-west to Deming and California, and on the east is the whole system of Texas Railroads.

Going back now to Rincon, in order to take the other branch of the A., T. & S. F. R. R., which leads to Deming, and ultimately by its extension, the Sonora Railroad, to Hermosillo, (Air-mo-seel'yo), and Guaymas (Give'mas), in Sonora, we find the only place worthy of mention between Rincon and Deming to be

Nutt, named after the well-known railroad official. While this town itself is small, it is important as being the station for Lake Valley, Kingston, etc.

Lake Valley is twelve miles distant, by stage, and is perhaps the most wonderful mineral locality for silver in the world. Here are the celebrated "Sierra" mines, and the unique and beautiful "Bridal Chamber," where much of the ore is worth from $8 to $10 per pound.

Hillsborough is a flourishing mining town, about eighteen miles north of Lake Valley; and about twenty miles north-west of the latter, and twelve miles from Hillsborough, by the road, lies

Kingston, the central town of the celebrated Percha Mining District, the discoveries in which made such an excitement in 1882.

Returning to the railroad again,

Deming is the junction of the A., T. & S. F. R. R. and the S. P. R. R. It was laid out in the spring of 1881, and is already a place of importance, but its railroad position assures it a large increase of prosperity and growth in the future. The Florida (Flo-ree'dah), Mountains, and the Tres Hermanos (Trace Air-mán-oce). Three Brothers, south of Deming, are both promising mining regions. The United States Custom-house is located here. At Deming passengers for Arizona, California, or Sonora, change cars to the Southern Pacific Railroad. The only point of importance on that railroad, in New Mexico, is

Lordsburgh, which is in the center of an important mining section, and the station for San Simon (San See-mon'e), and Shakspeare (which was formerly called Ralston).

Tourists in this direction should be sure to stop at

Tucson, to see the quaint Spanish town, and the singular church of San Javier (Have-e-air'), with its highly colored arabesque ornamentation. From Deming a narrow gauge railroad proceeds to

Silver City, which is the county seat of Grant County, and one of the most prosperous and progressive towns in the Territory. This city has been built entirely from the product of the mines in its vicinity; and while many of these are largely developed, new discoveries of importance are constantly made. The principal public buildings are the Court-house and the Public School, but the city abounds in fine business houses and private residences. The visitor should not fail to visit some of the principal mines and mining works while here. Those of Hon. M. W. Bremen are of world-wide reputation. From here stages run to

Georgetown, a thriving mining town about twenty miles north-west, and pass on the way the celebrated

Santa Rita Mines, which are the oldest and largest copper mines in the South-west. They were discovered in the year 1800 by Col. Carrisco, who soon after sold them to Don Francisco Manuel Elguea, a capitalist of Chihuahua. The copper was so pure that it was all bought by the Mexican government for coinage. The present works at these mines are very extensive.

The Old Hanover Mines are near at hand, and while not worked now, the ruins of the old smelters which were deserted on account of Indians, years ago, bear evidence to their extent.

The Atlantic & Pacific Railroad.

This railroad runs westerly from Albuqueque to California, following as nearly as practicable the 35° of latitude. It passes through a country of much interest to the tourist, both historically and scenically; and also through mineral regions of large extent—especially coal-fields sufficiently great to supply almost the whole nation.

The two Pueblo towns which are the most conspicuous in the early Spanish history are Zuñi (Soon'yee) and Acoma, known in Coronado's time as Cibola and Acuco. Cibola was the capital of the "Seven Cities," the glowing descriptions of which induced the first Spanish expeditions. Here Estevanico, the companion of Cabeza de Vaca, was killed in 1540, and Friar Marcos, while viewing the city from afar, did not dare enter it. The next year came Coronado, and besides visiting Zuñi, was the first European to see Acoma, built on its dizzy height, and almost inaccessible on account of the steepness of the ascent. This whole country is historic; and these two points alone are well worth a trip across the continent to visit. Both are reached from stations on the Atlantic & Pacific Railroad. On the line of the road itself is situated

Laguna, (Lah-goon'ah), one of the most populous and interesting Pueblo towns. It is the only remaining village of a populous province of natives which existed here 300 years ago. In 1882 a company of Territorial Militia was organized here, consisting entirely of **Pueblo Indians.**

Not far from Zuñi stands the Moro, or Inscription **Rock,** upon which are recorded the names of many distinguished travellers who have passed this way during three centuries, including Governors, Generals, and Bishops. North-west of Zuñi, in Arizona, are the

Moqui Villages, (Mo'kee) which, in 1540, constituted the Province of Totonteac, which Friar Marcos was told was the "most powerful kingdom in the world," and which are the least changed by time of any of the Pueblo towns.

In natural scenery this route is very rich. There are the volcanic craters in the San Mateo Mountains; the new "Garden of the Gods," near Chavez Station; those celebrated pieces of Nature's architecture, called the "Navajo Church," and Pyramid Rock, near Ft. Wingate; Clear Creek Cañon and the Cañon Diablo, both of great beauty; and crowning all, the Grand Cañon of the Colorado, too well known to need description, but which is, undoubtedly, the grandest natural wonder of the world.

The Denver & Rio Grande and Texas, Santa Fe & Northern R. R's., and country adjacent.

The Denver & Rio Grande R. R. enters the Territory just south of Antonito, and proceeds almost directly southerly to Española, thirty miles from Santa Fé, where it joins the T., S. F. & N. R. R., which makes the connecting link to Santa Fé.

From Antonito a branch of the D. & R. G. proceeds westerly, partly in New Mexico and partly in Colorado, to Durango and Silverton.

The principal points of interest on these routes, in New Mexico, starting from Santa Fé, are as follows:

San Yldefonso, (Eel-de-fon'e-so). This is an Indian pueblo, on the east bank of the Rio Grande, about twenty-two miles from Santa Fé. It is built around a plaza, in the usual style, most of the houses being two stories high. Fine fields surround the town; and the women of this pueblo are noted for their good looks, and, especially, brilliant eyes. This was a very important town when the Spaniards first arrived, and was the seat of the first Franciscan Monastery in the Territory. The Mesa, or flat-topped hill, just north of the pueblo, is a very conspicuous object for many miles, and for many generations was the rallying point for the northern Pueblos in all their wars; and in the time of the reconquest by Vargas, was the center around which most of the history of that long conflict revolves.

The church here is one of the oldest and most interesting in New Mexico. It is ninety feet long, and on the west side, surrounding a placita, are the buildings which were the cloisters of the Franciscan monks, long years ago. The roof of the church is made of the usual vigas, but instead of being covered with boards, the covering is made of small branches of willow or cottonwood, laid closely together, as is frequently seen in old buildings erected before saw-mills were introduced. Behind the altar are six large pictures, all painted on wood, the central one being of San Yldefonso. In the baptistery are three wooden "Santos"—images of Saints—of Mexican manufacture, and several old pictures, among which the tourist must not overlook one which is painted on a dressed buffalo-hide. This represents the earliest stage of art in the Territory, and paintings on this novel kind of canvas are very rare.

Santa Clara is an interesting pueblo on the west side of the Rio Grande, about three miles south of Española. There is an old church here well worth a visit.

Espanola, (Ace-pan-yo'lah), is the southerly terminus of the D. & R. G. R. R., and is a modern village, doing a flourishing business. Across the river from here, and only two miles distant, is

Santa Cruz, (San'tah Crooce), long the principal city of the Northern District of New Mexico, and the center in ecclesiastical affairs of the great parish of the north. This town was the head-quarters of the Revolution of 1837, and here the leaders were ultimately captured, and Gonzalez, the "Governor," shot. Close to this town also, was fought the principal battle between the Americans and the insurgents in the time of the "Taos Insurrection," known as the "Battle of La Cañada." The principal object of interest, however, is

The Great Church of Santa Cruz. This church is much the largest in the Territory, and is full of objects of interest to the antiquarian and the artist, as well as the devout Christian. The present edifice was built immediately after the reconquest of New Mexico by the Spaniards, under Vargas, about the year 1700. It is built in the usual form of a cross, consisting chiefly of the church proper and two chapels, one of Our Lady of Carmel on the north, and of San Francisco on the south, the sacristy and baptistery being behind the chapel of San Francisco, and another sacristy in front of the chapel of Our Lady of Carmel.

In the nave, until recently, were six very fine old Spanish paintings on one side, and an equal number of crude Mexican pictures just opposite, forming a most marked contrast. The former have now been placed in other positions. The Mexican pictures, which are still on the north side, consist of seven in all. The lower tier represents Our Lady of Sorrows, St. Joseph, and St. Stephen; above them is a representation of the crucifixion with a saint on each side, and surmounting all, a picture of Our Lady of Guadalupe.

On the opposite side, in a niche fifteen feet long by eight feet high, is a representation of Christ in the Tomb; and near it are two figures, one of Our Lord, and one of Our Lady of Carmel, the latter in an embroidered silk robe. Neither of these have artistic merit; but near them is the most beautiful specimen of antique wood carving in the Territory, being a statuette of St. Francis. It has, unfortunately, lost the hands, but is a most interesting example of Spanish seventeenth century art. The altar piece consists of a number of separate paintings. In the center is a statue of the Virgin and Child, and above them a large cross. On the south of the statue are pictures of Santa Teresa, with a dove, and St. Joseph and the Child; and on the north San Francisco Javier, and Santa Barbara. Above the former is a Holy Family, including San Joaquin and Santa Ana; and above the latter two angels. To the south of the altar is a picture of King Ferdinand; and on the north, St. Jerome.

In the chapel of St. Francis, sometimes called the chapel of the Penitentes, is a wooden statue of St. Francis three and one-half feet high, and a small Mexican picture of the nativity.

In the chapel of Our Lady of Carmel is a beautiful modern image of the Virgin, crowned; and on each side a painting on metal, one of St. Anthony of Padue, and one of St. Joseph. Behind the statue, and now hidden from view, is a picture of Our Lady of Carmel.

The doors which lead to this chapel are very curious, being made in elaborate panels, and painted blue, red, and yellow. In the sacristy attached to this chapel are a great many ornaments of Mexican manufacture, which, with the growth of a more refined taste, or from their becoming broken, have been discarded from time to time. Among them are two Angels of the Last Judgment, with long trumpets, said to have been made at Chimayó, and a number of paintings on wood, including a Holy Family, San Francisco, Señora of Guadalupe, etc. The walls of the chapels are four and one-half feet thick, and those of the church in some places still thicker.

In the main sacristy are several of the Spanish paintings which were originally in the nave of the church, and many other interesting articles. Among these are: Two companion pictures of large size—one of the Virgin and Child, and one of St. Joseph and the Child; the Archangel Gabriel; Our Lady of Sorrows; a smaller picture of San Joaquin; the Coronation of the Blessed Virgin by the Holy Spirit. All of these pictures are of artistic merit, and probably were brought from Spain at an early day. Several, and **especially** the last, bear evident traces of the school of Murillo. The Banner of the Confraternity of the Blessed Sacrament; two ancient candlesticks of tin, each eight feet high; **a baptismal font of beaten copper**, two feet in diameter, with a silver conch-shell; a batraca of **wood, used instead of a bell to call the** congregation during the last three **days of** Lent; **a pyx of solid silver**, heavily gilt; magnificent sacerdotal vestments embroidered in gold **and silver**.

Among the most interesting books preserved in this church are the following:—

1. "Libro de Casamientos de la Villa Nueva de Santa Cruz. Año 1726."

   Record of marriages of the new town of Santa Cruz. This was commenced by "Padre **Predicator** fray Manuel de Sopeña," and the frontispiece is a picture, in elaborate pen-and-ink work, **of the marriage** of the Blessed Virgin and St. Joseph.

2. Libro de Difuntos de la Mission de San Diego de los **Jemez.**

   The record of deaths at Jemez, beginning August, 1720. **This was kept by Father** Francisco C. J. Delgado, "**Notary of the Holy** Office of the Inquisition."

3. Record of deaths at Santa Cruz, 1726, with **three title-pages in** curious penwork.

   The books contain many interesting documents, as, for example, a letter from the King of Spain as to Indian affairs, in 1769.

   This church was the central seat of the Confraternity of **Our Lady of Carmel**, and contains a register of all of its members, "made by authority **of the Pope and** the Bishop of Durango." in 1760, and a curious record of **its property and expenses**, dated 1768.

   The Pueblo of San Juan (San Hwahn) is on the **east side of the** Rio Grande, **five miles above Santa** Cruz. It is a large town, surrounded by fertile fields, and the **seat of a large** manufactory of pottery. The Indians here also prepare bird-skins in a peculiar way, for ornaments. From the uniform loyalty of the people of this Pueblo **to the** Spaniards, it was named "San Juan de los Caballeros" (St. Jonn of the Gentleman).

   Plaza de Alcalde is a pleasant village three miles above San Juan, and was until 1880 the county seat of **Rio Arriba County.** Opposite here, at the junction of the Chama & Rio Grande, **is the historic spot where** Oñate founded the

   City of New Mexico, the first permanent settlement made by his expedition in 1592.

   La Joya (Lah Hoy'yah) **is a** charming spot on **the east bank, almost surrounded** by hills, and fields with peaches, apricots, and grapes. **From here commences** the U. S. military road to Taos, built along the east side of the Rio **Grande.**

   Embudo (Aim-boo'dah) is the station from which the stages **run to**

   Fernando de Taos (Touce).—This latter is **one of the** most interesting towns in the Territory. It is built around a plaza which was parked in 1881. Here were the first trading-places of the early pioneers. Roubidoux came here about 1822, and **Beaubien** six years later. Bent and St. Vrain had an establishment here, and Kit Carson made it his home and is buried here. The church is a large one, containing many **objects of interest,** and the tourist should not fail to see the old broken bell in the door-yard of the Padre. The **Sisters** of Loreto have a school here, kept by a **small number of devoted women;** and the Presbyterians also have a mission school. At the east end of the town is a chapel, generally known as the Penitente's Chapel, which contains several interesting and curious pictures. **The** key can generally be obtained from the lady who owns the property. The Penitentes are very numerous in this country, and have a *morada* or lodge-room east of the town in the valley. Here can be seen fifteen large crosses from sixteen to seventeen feet long, which they carry by way of penance in Holy Week, and especially **on Good Friday. It was at Taos** that Governor Bent and the other officials **were killed at** the outbreak **of what is** called the **"Taos Insurrection" in January, 1847.** Shortly afterwards, the American army, under Price, after the battle of Cañada and Embudo, appeared, **pursuing the** revolutionists, who had lost many of their number by the return of Mexicans to their homes, **and now largely consisted** of Pueblo Indians. **The latter entrenched themselves in the old** church at the **Taos Pueblo, and here a fierce battle took place, the** stronghold **finally being stormed and taken.** Montoya, **the chief in the revolutionary movement, and fourteen others—seven Mexicans and seven Pueblos—were executed** for participation **in the killing of Governor Bent, etc.**

Taos Pueblo is three miles from **the village of Taos, and is by far the most interesting** of the pueblos in the Rio Grande Valley. **It consists chiefly of two large buildings,** each five stories high, and **inhabited by about 350 persons. It is the best existing** example of the many-storied Pueblo houses, **as seen by the early discoverers, and no** one should come to the **South-west without visiting it. It has been rendered so familiar by pictures and descriptions that it seems unnecessary to say** more of it here.

El Rancho de Taos is a large town about four miles **south-east of Fernandez, and is** perhaps the best **example** of an unchanged **Mexican town to be found. It** has a **large** church, two or three very **ancient** houses; and near it is **a warm spring.**

North of Taos, distant twelve and twenty-four miles respectively, **are the**

Rio Hondo and Rio Colorado, (Ree'o Oan'do and Ree'o Cole-o-rah'do) both bordered by **large areas** of gold-bearing gravel, and the center **of well-known** mining **districts.**

About twenty-five miles south **of Taos, is the**

Pueblo of Picuris, (Pee-coo-réece) a small pueblo among the **mountains** of much **historic** interest. Near **here are** flourishing mining districts, **containing** gold, silver, copper, and iron; prominent, among the localities, **being Copper Mountain and Copper** Hill.

From Embudo the **railroad ascends by a very extraordinary grade to the mesa** on the west side of **the Rio Grande, which here passes through a deep cañon.**

Barranca is the station **from which stages run to**

Ojo Caliente, or Hot Springs, of Rio Arriba County. These have been celebrated for **a century or more.** Pike describes them in 1807. **There are four** springs, and they are strongly mineralized. The temperature is about 115°. An excellent hotel accommodates guests here. The Springs and adjoining property belong to Hon. Antony Joseph. On the hills above the Springs are the ruins of three pre-historic pueblos, and across the river are two more. These are full of interesting relics of the past, and the **lines of long rows of buildings can be easily distinguished.**

Tres Piedras (Trace Pe-ay'dras) is the **station for the mining district** which has the singular name of **Headstone.**

On the western branch from **Antonito the scenery is truly magnificent, culminating** in that of the celebrated

Toltec Gorge, around which the railroad **sweeps, giving splendid views of** this natural wonder. The railroad itself for forty miles **is a miracle of itself—winding** back and forth as it ascends the mountains, so that there is scarcely any point where the road is not visible from the car-windows on one side or the other; and at one **place** it passes the same spot three times.

The Cliff Dwellings and Cave Cities of the North-west are to be reached by this road. From Chama station **a road runs fifteen miles to**

Tierra Amarilla (Te-air'rah Am-ah-reel'ya), the **county seat of Rio**

Arriba County. Going down the valley of the Chama from here, and about half way back to Española, is the old town of

Abiquiu (Ah-bee-cue′), long the outpost of civilization on the Indian border. The town itself will interest the tourist, and it possesses an old church which will well repay a visit. Besides this, there are the ruins of an ancient pueblo about three miles below the town that will fully reward a day's examination.

The Tertio-Millennial Celebration, 1550-1883.

As the Three Hundred and Thirty-third Anniversary of the first European settlement of Santa Fé approached, a strong sentiment manifested itself in favor of having a suitable commemoration of such an important historic event.

This first took shape at a meeting of the Board of Trade, in the fall of 1882, when it was resolved to arrange for such a celebration; and soon after the "Santa Fé Tertio-Millennial Anniversary Association" was incorporated. Its directors, elected at the first annual meeting, are: Solomon Spiegelberg, L. B. Prince, W. V. Hayt, W. W. Griffin, W. T. Thornton, R. Martinez, E. L. Bartlett, A. Boyle, A. Seligman, A. Staab, L. Spiegelberg; and the officers are: President, W. W. Griffin; Vice-Presidents, L. B. Prince, A. Seligman, R. Martinez; Treasurer, L. Spiegelberg; Secretary, Arthur Boyle; with Charles W. Greene as General Manager.

The Association almost immediately decided that the celebration should take the double form of a historic commemoration, and an exhibition of the resources and productions of the Territory. The historic commemoration will consist of addresses by distinguished speakers on appropriate topics; of the reproduction by aboriginal tribes, both civilized and wild, of the ceremonies, dances, games, etc., of the Indian inhabitants; of historic pageants representing the great events of the past three centuries, from the coming of the first Spanish travellers and explorers until the present time, etc. With this view, by permission of the United States government, bands of Mescalero Apaches, of Navajoes, and of Pueblo Indians from Zuñi, Laguna, Santo Domingo, San Juan, Taos, San Yldefonso, etc., will be present; and leading citizens of both Spanish and American descent, have arranged to take part in the historic pageants.

The Exposition of resources and productions will probably include the finest display of mineral ever made at one time, including a great variety of ores of gold, silver, copper, lead, coal (anthracite and bituminous), etc., with mica, plumbago, cement, plaster-of-Paris, building stones, and other mineral products; wool of all kinds, and in every form; and the largest variety possible, so early in the season, of fruits and vegetables; besides manufactured products of various kinds.

The Association fortunately secured from the Government the fine square of land selected years ago for the Territorial Capitol, and have erected thereon the various buildings necessary. The main building is 480 feet long by 60 feet wide, and has been pronounced by those who are best informed in such matters to be the most perfect structure for its purpose ever erected—being lighted entirely from above by a uniform light, free from glare. Attached to the northern side of this is a large annex, which the great extent of the exhibits made necessary.

The old Capitol building, begun in 1859 but never finished, has been utilized by being floored, roofed, and supplied with windows and doors—thus making a very strong and convenient stone structure, which is used for a reception room for invited guests, offices of the Association, exhibition rooms for valuable antiquities, pictures, etc., etc.

For meetings, addresses, balls, concerts, etc., a great tent, capable of accommodating 3,000 persons, has been erected, over a smooth floor. All kinds of minor conveniences for the comfort of visitors are provided with care. A large building for a restaurant is near the front entrance. Other restaurants, refreshment-parlors, etc. are in various places on the grounds. A race-track, one-third of a mile long, surrounds the principal buildings. A charming lake is north-west of the Capitol building, and fountains abound on every hand. The Indians are encamped in four different parts of the grounds; and two regimental bands of the United States Army—those of the Thirteenth and Twenty-Fifth Regiments—through the courtesy of Major-General Pope, are to remain during the entire celebration.

It is useless to reproduce the programme here, as it is printed officially for distribution; but it may be said generally, that no such succession of attractions was ever before presented to the public—certainly not of such an interesting and instructive historic character.